ORDER AND DISORDER

*This is the fourth publication in the series
"Collected Writings of the Orpheus Institute"
edited by Peter Dejans*

Proceedings of the "International Orpheus
Academy for Music Theory 2003"

ORDER AND DISORDER

Music-Theoretical Strategies
in 20th-Century Music

Jonathan Dunsby
Joseph N. Straus
Yves Knockaert
Max Paddison
Konrad Boehmer

COLLECTED WRITINGS OF THE

ORPHEUS

INSTITUTE

Leuven University Press

2004

CONTENTS

PREFACE / P. 07

— Jonathan Dunsby
 Music-Analytical Trends of the Twentieth Century / P. 11

— Joseph N. Straus
 Atonal Composing-Out / P. 31

— Yves Knockaert
 Systemlessness in Music / P. 53

— Max Paddison
 Nature and the Sublime: The Politics of Order and Disorder in Twentieth-Century Music / P. 107

— Konrad Boehmer
 Music and Politics / P. 137
 Towards a Terza Prattica / P. 157

PERSONALIA / P. 169

COLOPHON / P. 175

PREFACE

Between April 9 and 13, 2003, the Orpheus Institute in Ghent (Belgium) staged its first-ever "International Orpheus Academy for Music Theory", where five respected guest lecturers met professional music theorists, musicologists and musicians from various European and American countries.

The motto of this first "Orpheus Academy" were 20th-century music and theory, especially after the 1950s. Theoretical, historical and philosophical aspects were discussed and confronted with performance practice.

The five guest lecturers tackled different subjects, with the explicit request that the audience ask questions and discuss what had been said.

We were honored to welcome the following guest lecturers at the 2003 edition of our "International Orpheus Academy for Music Theory": Konrad Boehmer (NL), Jonathan Dunsby (UK), Yves Knockaert (B), Max Paddison (UK) and Joseph N. Straus (US).

The present "Proceedings" of our first Orpheus Academy do not contain the complete texts of the lectures held last year: some authors indeed decided to publish only one of their lectures, while others combined the contents of their presentations to one long text. We are confident, though, that this book nevertheless provides an interesting overview of the subjects that were covered between April 9 and 13, 2003 at the Orpheus Institute in Ghent.

In *Music-Analytical Trends of the Twentieth Century*, Jonathan Dunsby discusses key features in the development of music analysis from pre-structuralist to postmodern times, examining its shifting role as compositional theory, as discourse in historical musicology, and as an autonomous discipline of musical understanding.

The mediated, complex relationship of theory to compositional practice and to the history of ideas in this period is explored with reference to writings by, among others, Adorno, Agawu, Babbitt, Bernard, Boretz, Boulez, Nattiez, Webern, and Whittall.

In *Atonal Composing-Out*, Joseph N. Straus discusses ways in which the intervallic and motivic ideas of the musical surface are projected over larger spans. Atonal music has two principal ways of achieving this rapport among the structural levels: the projection of motivic intervals or sets within contextual lines defined by register or contour, and the projection of motives along transformational paths, usually involving transposition or inversion of pitch-class sets or other discrete musical elements.

In the article *Systemlessness in Music*[1], Yves Knockaert investigates the controllability of non-intention — whether or not Cage used coincidence in a purely unsystematic way — , the compositional approach of Morton Feldman's 'floating thoughts', and the 'raw state' (*Rohzustand*) of Wolfgang Rihm's music of the 1980s. Knockaert tries to find out why those composers decided to work without a system, and what the consequences of that decision were for their aesthetic considerations in music.

In *Nature and the Sublime: The Politics of Order and Disorder in Twentieth-Century Music*, Max Paddison exposes a history of the concept of nature in relation mainly to music of the first half of the twentieth century, with some reference also to literature and the visual arts. This context is developed to discuss the concept of the sublime with particular emphasis on music of the second half of the century. A point of reference will be Lyotard's assertion in discussing Kant's Analytic of the Sublime: "The sublime denies the imagination the power of forms, and denies nature the power to immediately affect thinking with forms".

Finally, Konrad Boehmer, in *Music and Politics*[2], does not pursue the old discussion of 'music for the working class', a discussion

---

1. The original title of this text was "Systeemloosheid in de nieuwe muziek. Componeren zonder systeem: denkwijze en werkwijze. Een vergelijkend onderzoek naar systeemloosheid in het werk van John Cage, Morton Feldman en Wolfgang Rihm."
2 The original title of this text was "Musik und Politik".

preface

loved by composers of the '68 generation. Instead, he analyses several aspects of the political economy of music, in the hope that they not only reveal what is going on, but that they also hint at perspectives for the future. In his second essay, *Towards a Terza Prattica*, Konrad Boehmer calls electric music a 'terza prattica', based on Monteverdi's concept of 'prima' and 'seconda prattica'. After (medieval) vocal polyphony (about 1000–1600) and instrumental music (about 1600–1950), a new era seems to have begun, where electricity is emerging as the third productive force of European art music, based on biological and mechanical principles. Thus, a fundamental change in the compositional paradigm is heralded, which looks as radical as the transition from feudal and theological polyphony to bourgeois music of representation. The essay mainly focuses on the (possible) perspectives of this paradigmatic change.

I would like to seize the opportunity to thank my co-editors Frank Agsteribbe and Sylvester Beelaert, and all those who have contributed to the realisation of this publication.

Peter Dejans

MUSIC-ANALYTICAL TRENDS OF THE TWENTIETH CENTURY

Jonathan Dunsby

1. INTRODUCTION

1.1.

I thought it would be worthwhile to begin this introduction with something topical, and looking at recent specialist literature I fell upon a recent issue of *Music Theory Spectrum* in which the editor seeks to explain the publication of a number of articles on pitch-class networks. This explanation is expert and tasteful but it also involves some small degree of rhetoric, where Daniel Harrison defends a position. In particular, he talks of how a discipline—music theory—"feeds itself"; and also of how "theorists not only originate but also consolidate" (Harrison 2002: 163). I do not think there is anything necessarily wrong with these aspects so long as they remain just that—aspects, rather than the sole justification. It is perfectly obvious, after all, that for an activity to be coherent, to be enhanced by the sharing of ideas both critical and purposeful, to be able to have an awareness, in short, of its own history, that is, to be a discipline, then such an activity will be to some extent self-sustaining and, to use Harrison's word, it will 'consolidate'. In a very much more sophisticated context, this is one consequence also of Thomas Christensen's reminder towards the end of his essay "Music Theory and its Histories" that "from a hermeneutic perspective all analytical activity is fully historical" (Christensen 1993: 32).

1.2.

If we allow some provisional validity to the idea of consolidation, and historicity, this is nevertheless no magic lever to unlock a mechanism that unrolls for inspection what we are calling here the analytical 'trends' of the last hundred-or-so years. There is no 'smooth' story to be told, in my opinion; and this is for at least three reasons.

1.2.1.

First is the epistemological level. What kind of knowledge is music-analytical knowledge? I am of course saying nothing remotely new if I divide the answer into its practices, claiming that

- music analysis can constitute or complement a theory of musical composition;
- that analysis is also a particular mode of discourse within historical musicology and, to some extent, within systematic musicology, if we are to accept Adler's hallowed account from 1885 of the scope, method and aim of musicology (see Bujić 1988: 348–55);
- and that analysis is an autonomous discipline of musical understanding, something worthwhile in and of itself as part of the enlarging of the individual consciousness of each of us (see Dunsby 1992).

From this perspective, it is hardly surprising that what appears to be knowledge to some may seem to be mere word-play to others. Even without reference to the empirical constraints that I shall be mentioning shortly, purely in the abstract world as it were of what analysis thinks it is trying to tell us, there will be inevitable barriers, not disagreements even, but genuine and justifiable failures to see the point.

1.2.2.

Secondly, the art of composing music during this period has been diverse, to say the least, and I thoroughly recommend Arnold Whittall's new book *Exploring Twentieth-Century Music*, both because of its commanding focus on that diversity, and also because it offers an evidence-based approach to music history that cannot but be of great interest to those with a sympathy for music-analytical insight (Whittall 2003). Not only have there been two distinct phases of so-called 'modernism' in the early and in the mid twentieth century, but there have been certain quantum leaps in technology, which is an optional creative resource perhaps, but one which becomes an integral cultural force once it has been used; there has been what cultural historians called at one time popularisation; and in recent years we have become acutely aware of the effects of what the sociologist Anthony Giddens was one of the first to theorize — 'globalisation' (Giddens 1999). It is no accident that what may be called 'mainstream' musicology has become in some areas almost obsessed with the idea of 'canonicity' (see for example Bergeron and Bohlman 1992) at a time of what we perceive as unprecedented and somewhat bewildering cultural activity and dissemination. And so it goes on. As Arnold Whittall writes:

> At the end of the twentieth century, serious art music is still modern, still plural, its classicising potential still strong, its radical inheritance continually reasserted and continually questioned, while its need to relate to aspects of the wider world, like ethnic identity and technological advance, remains undiminished. (Whittall 1999: 392)

1.2.3.

Alongside and to some extent crossing through this — in other words, as set against the fairly comprehensible forces of epistemological and cultural diversity — is, thirdly, the sheer human contingency of human discourse. Admittedly, we could simply aggregate all examples of such contingency in some category of hapax, as things we just do not know about in the sense of being able to generalize about them. I would like to illustrate this, in order to raise almost from the beginning some more technical issues, by brief comment on the history of pitch-class set theory. The theory of pitch has always been at a premium in core aspects of twentieth-century composition and theory, in much the same way that we find it stretching back through previous centuries. All the way from Schoenberg's prediction that one day people would work out the bases of atonal harmony, through Babbitt's mid-century assertions about the primacy of pitch among the domains of musical invention, right up to the present and, if I may mention it, the specific invitation of the Orpheus Institute that this symposium include discussion of 'non-pitch' parameters, composers have been concerned about where the next note comes from, and theorists have wanted to rediscover either the historical truth of answers to that question or contemporaneous perceptual answers to it. We are all familiar with the faltering history of the early days of dodecaphonic analysis, including ludicrous if understandable technical claims, alongside claims that were aesthetically suspect such as the question of how Schoenberg had come to make what is without doubt a serial error in the Op. 33a *Klavierstück*. It became as clear, later, that this 'science' really had made progress as it had previously been doubtful: for there was much to be learned from, say, Martha Hyde's work on Schoenberg's dodecaphonic practice especially in light of the sketch materials (Hyde 1992), and certainly Kathryn Bailey's study of Webern's music (Bailey 1992) provided a vademecum that one might need alongside, say, one's guide to Wagner's Leitmotives (not that anybody would want to make too much of that comparison). The history of pitch-class set theory was at least equally faltering, and probably much more so, since it was never so clear what the questions were in the first place. Jonathan Bernard produced a virtuosic account of this history, in which he faced the difficult task of describing failure in an interesting way:

> It is a peculiar history in many ways, hardly a straightforward linear progression: full of duplicated effort, reinventings of the wheel, and seemingly inexplicable conceptual leaps. Perhaps most unexpected is the definite impression that begins to form as to the lack of inevitability about the emergence of the pc set, that as late as mid-century the tendency toward comprehensive accounting for pitch combination in the twelve-note universe might have led to a very different result by the 1960s than the one that actually came about. (Bernard 1997: 12)

Bernard argued that the development of pitch-class set theory was surprisingly repertoire-driven — to which one might respond that on the one hand this is not really any great surprise given the intense focus of its avatars, Milton Babbitt and David Lewin in particular, on particular spots of modern Western musical culture; and on the other hand it was also significantly driven not by repertoire but by developments in contemporary thinking, in mathematics especially, and not least in technology, since central aspects of twentieth-century pitch theories would have been no more possible with the use of a slide-rule than they would have been with Napier's bones, and the extreme sceptic might see such theories as ways of using the computer largely because electronic computation was there to be used rather than answering anyone's prayers. In other words, to return to the idea put forward in this third category of theory's lack of a 'smooth' story, we have human contingency, as the hapax if we find it to be a largely random and unconvincing phenomenon, or as some sort of thing-in-itself if we find it to carry truth-content.

1.3.

We also have to reckon with the fact that 'consolidation' is anything but a replete characterization of all that music theory and analysis in respect of the music of the last hundred years is for and about. On the contrary, it is a common desire among theorists, whether implicitly or explicitly, to enrich and inevitably in some sense to supplement musical practice pure and simple.

1.3.1.

Very often, it has to be said, this amounts to aspiration rather than demonstrable fact. I have mentioned Bailey's Herculean work on Webern, but in general one may ask that when one thinks of whatever one considers to be a highlight of musical composition of the last hundred years, *in which cases does one also think of an explanation of it*, a commentary, a contextualization? This question is simplistic, naturally, since art does not rely on criticism for validation, or not in any unmediated way, and it is also an introversive question since just the same could be asked of any of the great works of visual and plastic art in the Tate Modern, or of modern poetry, or even of film. Yet in another aspect, the aspect in which you can legitimately take a specialist interest in these matters, it is actually rather an interesting question. Undoubtedly, certain acts of music criticism become part of the legacy of the work's identity: on detail, think of the opening of Schoenberg's First String Quartet, for example, enshrined in Berg's essay on the difficulty of understanding Schoenberg's music (Berg 1924); for a more general case, think of Ulrich Siegele's writing on Boulez's *Le marteau sans maître* (Siegele 1979). It is rather invidious anyway to pick out particular examples. No-one in their right mind would claim, I trust, that commentary on music of the last hundred years that calls itself theoretical, analytical, or just technically specific, has been undesirable or largely unsuccessful. We do however need to pay attention continually to those ways in which it can be said to offer a surplus, either by its accuracy and thoroughness or, if we are lucky, by its originality. You might judge, with justification, that this is a rare occurrence.

1.3.2.

I feel that it was Pierre Boulez above all who articulated the ways in which musical commentary may supplement musical practice. In the first place, or so it seems to me, he tends much more towards my third category of analysis — analysis as an autonomous discipline — than towards thinking of analysis as fundamentally oriented towards compositional theory, and much less in his case does analysis figure as the discourse of historical musicology. Especially in his lecture on "The Teacher's Task", originally from 1961, he expresses in his trenchant and memorable way the extent to which ideally thinking about music means thinking about oneself, not self-indulgently, but in relation to the truth-content of the work of art:

> A composition is sometimes no more than an excuse for introspection. The ultimate object of analysis is self-definition by the intermediacy of another ... this is the kind of investigation that I try to inculcate in my pupils. In a word, I want them to reach a point at which the masters of an earlier age speak to them about themselves. It is not an impossible ambition; and indeed I feel convinced that it is the quickest way to acquaint pupils with their own powers. Using this double-sided mirror of analysis, I try to give their technique greater precision by means of criticism, self-criticism in fact, and that is not always easy! (Boulez 1986: 123)

There, Boulez is talking principally about people's powers of composition and the way in which this can be nurtured through music study, but in my favourite passage from his essay "The Composer as Critic" his natural inclination towards the sheer joy of understanding for its own sake comes to the fore, and he sets an agenda for the best kind of criticism that most people, armed with appropriate humility, may well believe it best to leave to others to follow:

> The only really effective critic will be one who is capable of directing and sustaining a reflected image, and the vitality of his criticism will be determined by the deformations arising from the personal quality of his vision. Bar-by-bar accounts of a work are suspect, it is true; but there is a transcendent kind of criticism that is based on technical analysis, no doubt, but reveals such a mastery of the vocabulary that it can afford the generalization and syntheses forbidden to the short-sighted. (Boulez 1986: 109)

What this reinforces, at the same time as setting the highest possible hurdle in terms of standards of conviction and originality, is the value of theory as theory, the value of the ability to generalize and synthesize, and put in those ways it is easy to see the underlying unity of Boulez's vision, since his compositional aesthetic is bound up with exactly such concerns, as is well known. And what it means is that a prospect for analysis such as Adorno's, at least as expressed in 1968 in the Berg monograph, would not be enough for Boulez: for analysis to be both 'possible and conceivable' is, Adorno says, "the hidden basis for the whole idea of musical analysis: to grasp the artistic essence of music, its eloquence, its name, by way of technical facts" (Adorno 1991: 39). But Boulez was always asking for more; even just at the conversational level delightfully recorded in their 1965 "Discussions about *Pierrot lunaire*" this interplay surfaces where Boulez is looking for a surplus compared with Adorno—in respect of musical commentary of course, not of philosophy, and by the way I certainly do not mean to criticize Adorno, whose clarity over the purposes and requirements of analytical discourse is second to none (Adorno and Boulez 2001).

2. FROM PRE-STRUCTURALIST TO POSTMODERN

2.1.

I can assume that there will be general agreement on that 'pre-structuralist' implies: from the period of musical composition when there was not such an overt and publicly-discussed concern with theory and method, with intention and audience. Historians tend to link an onset of crisis, as 'constructivism' overwhelmed pre-structuralist habits, essentially with the exhaustion—it seemed to many—of major-minor tonality, and I think that is the right emphasis; for it would surely be bizarre to suppose that the *Diabelli Variations* were 'planned' with any less painstaking and indeed conscious care than went into masterpieces of earlier 20th-century music. The extent to which a characterization of some 20th-century musical composition as 'structuralist' is sustainable can be debated, but certainly musicology went through a readily-diagnosable structuralist phase, a long one, in which notions of cultural standards gave way to relativist arguments, to the analysis of self-reflexive interrelationships—an adjunct of which is the quaint idea that one should somehow analyse a piece of music 'on its own terms', a sentiment to be found decade after decade in musical discourse of the last century, especially in discourse that was antagonistic towards music-theoretical trends of the period. If so much can be agreed, the question of how postmodernism eventually figured in the history of music must remain open. Even the gurus of cultural theory are uncertain about it. It is amusing to read Christopher Butler's slight slip of expression when he hovers on the same page between apologetic extremes: "*the most* one can say", he writes, "is that, like the postmodernists, composers were often obsessed with the nature and function of language"; on the other hand, "*at the very least* much musical composition since 1970, notably in the extraordinary willingness to mix styles of younger composers, has avoided some of the dialectical battles of the past" (Butler 2002: 76; my emphasis). What is abundantly clear, however, is that postmodernism has been a celebration of the questioning of culture and of theorizing about it. It ought to have been really fertile ground for the growth of music theory.

2.2

I cannot resist the temptation to place together here two quotations. I would defend to the hilt the fact that they are taken out of context; it would be no great exercise of scholarship or argument to demonstrate that both are representative of the essence of their authors' positions, beliefs and rhetoric. The first is pithy, typical of the literary conceits of which its author is so fond and at which, let it be said, he is consistently rather good, if good means defensible and memorable:

[a] Language cannot capture musical experience because it cannot capture any experience whatever, including the experience of language itself.

The second is just a little longer, and again typical of its author, in this case in not stinting on detail and emphasis:

[b] In speech the sound is only a sign, that is, a means to an end which is entirely distinct from that means, while in music the sound is an object, i.e., it appears to us as an end in itself. The autonomous beauty of tone-forms in music and the absolute supremacy of thought over sound as merely a means of expression in spoken language are so exclusively opposed that a combination of the two is a logical impossibility.

We could spend a little time contemplating the relationship between these two: contemplating whether, for example, the second in fact contradicts the first in that language's inability to capture experience gives it something in common, reciprocally, with music, which obviously cannot capture the experience of language; or we could contemplate whether the first statement undermines the second by asserting a prior quality of language that makes it not 'opposed' to music as the second author would have it, but categorically distinct, just as, say, ducks and illnesses are distinct and bear no useful comparison with music, certainly not an oppositional comparison implying some form of meaningful dialectic. I should reveal, however, that the second quotation was actually written about 140 years before the first. It is a classic of pre-structuralist theory, at least if we are to agree with Jean-Jacques Nattiez that Hanslick, writing here in 1854, was asking questions that are still relevant and that were in effect too subtle to baldly assert musical autonomy; and for all that Hanslick seems to have wished to assert the autonomy of music and of musical structure, his depth of thought led him constantly away from this (Nattiez 1993). Hanslick's strict antinomy between language and music (for the above quotation 'b' see Hanslick 1986: 42) was but one of a series of heuristic devices that taken on their own either dissolve or are uninteresting. The first quotation, however, about language's utter dissociation from experience, is in the context of a discussion of 'Postmodernism and Musicology' (Kramer 1995: 1–32; 18), where Lawrence Kramer invites us, as I understand it, to abandon the categorical distinctions, the 'universal principles' of 'formalism and positivism' (: 33), in favour of an altogether more personally-oriented musicology (these are my words) where the 'alterity' of the self is, in the Zeitgeist of the 1980s, a pervasive, awe-inspiring totem.

2.3.

It would be all too easy, in the wake of that little comparison from the mid-19th century and the late-20th, to throw up one's hands in despair at the attempt to discern some sense of historical development in musicology broadly viewed, and in its sub-disciplines broadly viewed. What, we might ask, really is pre-structuralist about early 20th-century analysis, and what is so postmodern about its latest manifestations? Even if those are not thought to be useful terms, still one may believe that the theorist must never lose a sense of history, just as history must not lose its sense of theory. Precisely such a potential disjuncture has been diagnosed by Kofi Agawu in his much-discussed essay on "Analyzing Music under the New Musicological Regime", which repays careful study (Agawu 1996). The charge against analysis in the late-20th century was indeed one of 'formalism', as described by Agawu:

> The charge of formalism was made because analysts inquired only into the connections between patterns within a piece; they did not deal with matters of affect and expression, with the 'meaning' of music, with its cultural context. This unfortunate misrepresentation of a hitherto complex theoretical enterprise made possible the prescription of an instant cure. To escape the dilemmas of formalism, you must attach the patterns you have observed to something else: a plot, a program, an emotional scenario, a context, an agenda, a fantasy, or a narrative. You must, in other words, problematize the gap between the musical and the extra-musical. (: [5])

What critics of the theory 'establishment' were missing, Agawu reminds us, is that

> Within the discipline of theory, there exists a vast range of innovative inquiries that have been overlooked by new musicologists. Were it not for theorists' reticence about adopting new slogans, these initiatives would easily converge into a 'New Theory'. New musicologists' failure to acknowledge this work does not, of course, deny it a place in the discourses of the musical sciences. It only testifies to a willed amnesia on their part, a necessary strategy, perhaps, for redrawing the boundaries of the musical disciplines. (: [16])

Agawu goes on to mention work on the phenomenology of analysis, on network approaches, readings inspired by post-war French literary criticism, 'plural unities', Schenker revisions, semiotics, and discourse analysis. What he does not say, however, in so far as I can read along and also carefully in between his lines, is that analysis, postmodern though he rightly wants us to believe it to be in respect of its intellectual affiliations, engages in this postmodern environment with the music of its postmodern times. This is to say that although Agawu is right in principle, in practice everything in the theory garden is not necessarily rosy, if there are expectations of cultural growth and sustenance appearing there. There is even some irony perhaps in Agawu's comment that the commitment of music's analysts and theorists to technical demonstration "is sometimes facilely dismissed as an outgrowth of a modernist impulse" (: [22]): it is perhaps for another day to examine the question of whether the 'facile' nature of that dismissal is not also marking a crisp recognition among musicologists that theory not only tends to stick within its own landscape but is often uncomfortable with and in its own cultural present, as recognized in Schoenberg's acquiescent admission that theorizing the music of present must be for the future, and in Edward Cone's repeated recommendation that new music should wait about a decade before the theorists have a go at it (see for example Dunsby 1994: 85).

3. BERG, PRÄLUDIUM, DREI ORCHESTERSTÜCKE, OP. 6

3.1

It will be interesting, I hope, to examine briefly some comments on a composition first completed in 1914 — so more or less at the start of our period—which bears many of the hallmarks of (1) pre-structuralism and (2) postmodernism. By this I mean for instance

(1)

- that if this is not, after all, a twelve-note composition, it is nevertheless overtly 'planned', palindromically, as is indicated roughly by the tempo markings in bars 42 and 49, which refer to the 'corresponding' tempi of bars 9 and then 8–6 respectively (and I shall return to this palindromic structure);
- and also that its sound-world is highly differentiated even to the extent of what in 1968 Adorno calls, referring specifically at least to the sustained chord from bar 9, "a technical *rule*: no two notes of the same timbral family may be direct neighbors in a vertical construction" (Adorno 1991: 78; my emphasis);

and (2)

- that Berg is 'mixing', to use that favoured affect of postmodernism, the luxuriant extravagances of the Romantic symphonic world, through the Wagnerian instrumentation for example, with his modernistic taste for the aphoristic in phrasing, form and duration;
- and also that there is a kind of collage principle here as the music emerges unpitched out of silence, an effect that drives Adorno into a lyrical description of its relationship to cultural overthrow—"the beginning", he says, "belongs to the sphere of primitivism, as a strictly musical correlate of verbal-optical Dadaism" (: 76).

3.2.

In fact the palindromic structure of this piece is clearly what commentators of a certain generation and turn of mind found so remarkable here, Adorno writing in the 1960s towards the end of his life, and Dominique Jameux in a commentary that appeared only recently in his major study of Second Viennese music (Jameux 2002), but which in this case derives from material he originally published in *Musique en jeu* back in 1976. Adorno characteristically relates the opening of the Prelude to its sociological place: "Pure noise is the residual value of the subjective musical atom against the extra-musical reality of commodities; the strictest and, admittedly, expressionless form of banality and thus the transformation of pure expression into objectivity" (: 76). Jameux, not himself hesitant to wax lyrical about Berg's idea, with a brief discussion of how the music sinks back into the 'inorganic', then silence, and how in a handful of bars the composer forges and illustrates a veritable 'myth' through melody-as-metaphor of musical creativity itself (: 299–300), nevertheless also takes the trouble to provide a technical account of the retrogression in this music, from a conventional formal point of view at least, as shown in Figure 1:

Fig. 1

Berg, *Präludium, Drei Orchesterstücke*, Op. 6

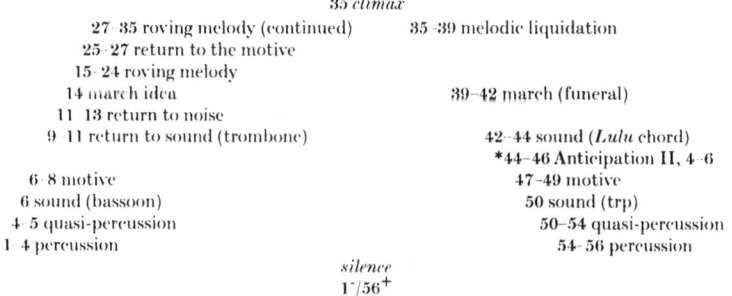

[Jameux 2002: 300; * alignment corrected]

3.3.

Although Jameux's analytical chart of Berg's Prelude is undoubtedly worthwhile, I also want to highlight the sense in which this kind of focus is also frustrating. Outlining the palindromic features of the music is after all the easiest thing to do. This static, diachronic picture is but one aspect of whatever it is that provides the magical line taking us through Berg's piece. Even Adorno, such an astute observer of musical continuity, cannot but resort to what I may be forgiven for calling weak, unimaginative metaphors of musical motion, as he discusses how ideas are 'taken up' or how a musical idea 'continues', is 'superimposed', or 'added', and the like (: 77) — and by the way this has nothing to do with issues of translation.

3.4

Is it any wonder, one may ask, that there has been a tendency towards the decisive in the analytical trends we are discussing? Can one fail to understand the synchronic urge that led the Americans in particular to take the synchronic axis as seriously as possible at least in terms of the domain — pitch — that as we have said has always been at a premium and inevitably so? Is there not an air of inevitability for example in the relatively recent transfer of pitch-class set preoccupations onto synchronic diatonic ones, a trend pioneered by such as Richmond Browne and John Clough, the latter having published extensively in this area (see, recently, Clough et al. 1999), and tending to be applied to the more conventional types of post-tonal diatonic expression (e.g. Santa 2000), but also being used in the study of, say, Steve Reich (Quinn 2002), and ripe for extrapolation? And how could anyone misunderstand the intentions of research by those who have been called the Neo-Schenkerians, with their compulsion to build models of the diachronic continuity of music that cries out for an understanding of how one gets from A to B, and especially — if I may put it this way, emblematically for so much music of the twentieth century — getting from A to B in a context where B turns out to be another version of A!? It does seem to me that this kind of perspective makes the customary condemnation of American post-war theory pretty much beside the point. Yes, it is true that as Nicholas Cook says it adopted "scientific language and symbol systems" to some extent. It is probably also true that in certain quarters "intuition and emotionally loaded language were ruthlessly eliminated" (Cook 1998: 96), although I would say science and symbol were also one of their most powerful affective representations, given that intuiting systems and trying to eviscerate language are among the most transparently emotion-laden of human activities, as we see in modern times with the desperate and utterly facile attempts to apply intellectual and forensic political attitudes to customary, brutal war-waging. The fact remains however that not one of the cultural ideas of the twentieth century has deliberately pointed away from the study of music as autonomous craft. Those who subscribed to what used to be called 'new musicology' — a term coined, interestingly enough, not by any American scholar but by Jean-Jacques Nattiez — may have largely, sadly turned away from contemporary art, but not from contemporary ideas.

4. CONCLUSION

4.1.

Of course, such microscopic slants on musical structure are reflections of macroscopic tendencies in any case. It may well be that today's generation of music theorists underestimates the would-be revolution that, as it were, failed to take place in the final third of the twentieth century, when modernism was no longer actually new, when perhaps there was an opportunity to see how it had found its place. One may even speculate that we are in the middle of its abandonment, only we fail to see that clearly precisely because this is going on around us: "it is possible to imagine", writes Arnold Whittall, a "twenty-first century striving to learn from the twentieth by rejecting it, lock, stock, and barrel, in order to secure the total and final demise of anything that might be thought of as avant-garde" (Whittall 1999: 392). The claims made for modernism, and consequently the responsibilities supposedly placed upon theorists and analysts of modernism, were extreme. In his 1976 essay on "Listening", for instance, Roland Barthes trundled along pulling his critical band-wagon with astonishing hyperbole even by his own brilliant standards: listening to compositions by John Cage, he says:

> it is each sound one after the next that I listen to, not in its syntagmatic extension, but in its raw and as though vertical *signifying*: by deconstructing itself, listening is externalised, it compels the subject to renounce his 'inwardness'. That is valid ... for many other forms of contemporary art, from 'painting' to the 'text'; and this, of course, does not proceed without some laceration, for no law can oblige the subject to take his pleasure where he does not want to go (whatever the reasons

might be for his resistance), no law is in a position to constrain our listening: freedom of listening is as necessary as freedom of speech. (Barthes 1991: 259-60)

Really? Apart from the journalistic agglomeration of Cage's works into a single object, to which any specialist is likely to object who actually knows Cage's music or most of it, what is it that Barthes is so afraid of in himself? Why feel 'compelled' to renounce one's 'inwardness' by art that exerts such a compulsion only by virtue of one's cultural introversiveness? — that is to say, if Cage's music really did come from Mars, as Barthes may as well be supposing, then we would probably eagerly take its verticality for granted while hunting ardently for some form of syntagmatic, diachronic understanding, and not least through poietic information from the composer or the circumstances of production, as well as from all kinds of neutral analysis.

4.2.

With the phrase 'all kinds of ... analysis' I am more than happy to betray my own, personal understanding of the right attitude to the remarkable phenomenon we are learning about here. It is impossible to predict what the next generation will be concerned about, and the concerns of the last generation are of interest to us only in so far as they have endured wholesale or at least in some recognizable form. In the present however it is of course extremely difficult to tease out what is really happening, 'really' meaning those aspects which within our own lifetimes we shall come to see as having had gravitas, as slotting in to key points of the jigsaw puzzle. That is one way to underline the seriousness of Christensen's dictum — open to discussion and refutation of course — that "all analytical activity is fully historical". One can think one knows what he means.

REFERENCES

Adorno, T., 1991: *Alban Berg: Master of the Smallest Link*, trans. J. Brand and C. Hailey, Cambridge, CUP
Adorno, T., and Boulez, P., 2001:
"Gespräche über den *Pierrot lunaire*", in: *Musik-Konzepte*, 112/113,

	July ('Schönberg und der Sprechgesang'), pp. 73–94
Agawu, K., 1996:	"Analyzing Music under the New Musicological Regime", in: *Music Theory On-Line*, 2/4, May, [accessed 29 March 2003]
Bailey, K., 1992:	*The Twelve-note Music of Anton Webern: Old Forms in a New Language*, Cambridge, CUP
Berg, A., 1924:	"Warum ist Schönbergs Musik so schwer verständlich?", in: *Musikblätter des Anbruch*, August/September, 8/8, pp. 329–41. English translation as "Why is Schoenberg's Music So Hard to Understand", in: E. Schwartz and B. Childs (eds), *Contemporary Composers on Contemporary Music*, New York, Da Capo Press, 1967, pp. 59–71; originally in: *The Music Review*, 13/2, May 1952, pp. 187–96.
Bergeron, K., and Bohlman, P. et al., eds, 1992:	*Disciplining Music: Musicology and its Canons*, Chicago, The University of Chicago Press
Bernard, J., 1997:	"Chord, Collection, and Set in Twentieth-Century Theory", in: James Baker et al. (eds), *Music Theory in Concept and Practice*, Rochester, University of Rochester Press, pp. 11–51
Boulez, P., 1986:	*Orientations: Collected Writings*, ed. J.-J. Nattiez, London, Faber
Bujić, B., ed., 1988:	*Music in European Thought 1851–1912*, Cambridge, CUP
Butler, C., 2002:	*Postmodernism: A Very Short Introduction*, Oxford, OUP
Christensen, T., 1993:	"Music Theory and its Histories", in: *Music Theory and the Exploration of the Past*, ed. C. Hatch and D. Bernstein, Chicago, The University of Chicago Press, pp. 9–39
Clough, J., Engebretsen, N., and Kochavi, J.:	"Scales, Sets, and Interval Cycles: A Taxonomy", in: *Music Theory Spectrum*, Spring, 21/1, pp. 74–104
Cook, N., 1998:	*Music: A Very Short Introduction*, Oxford, OUP
Dunsby, J., 1992:	"Music Analysis: Commentaries", in: John Paynter et al. (eds), *Companion to Contemporary Musical Thought*, London, Routledge, pp. 634–49
—, 1994:	"Criteria of Correctness in Music Theory and Analysis", in: A. Pople (ed.), *Theory, Analysis and Meaning in Music*, Cambridge, CUP, pp. 77–85
Giddens, A., 1999:	*Runaway World: How Globalisation is Reshaping our Lives*, London, Profile
Hanslick, E., 1986:	*On the Musically Beautiful: A Contribution towards the Revision of the Aesthetics of Music*, trans. G. Paysant, Indianapolis, Hackett Publishing Company
Harrison, D., 2002:	'From the Editor', *Music Theory Spectrum*, 24/2, Fall, pp. 163–4
Hyde, M., 1982:	*Schoenberg's Twelve-Tone Harmony: The Suite Op. 29 and the Compositional Sketches*, Ann Arbor, UMI Research Press
Jameux, D., 2002:	*L'Ecole de Vienne*, Paris, Fayard
Kramer, L., 1995:	*Classical Music and Postmodern Knowledge*, Berkeley, University of California Press
Nattiez, J.-J., 1993:	"Hanslick ou les apories de l'immanence", *Le combat de Chronos et d'Orphée*, Paris, Bourgois, 55–80
Quinn, I., 2002:	"Foundations of Steve Reich's Later Harmonic Practice: The *Variations* (1979) and *Tehillim* (1981)", paper at the Society for

	Music Theory Annual Meeting, Columbus, OH
Santa, M., 2000:	"Post-Tonal Diatonic Music: A Mod7 Perspective", in: *Music Analysis*, 19/2, July, pp. 167–201
Siegele, U., 1979:	*Zwei Kommentare zum 'Marteau sans maître' von Pierre Boulez*, Neuhausen-Stuttgart, Hänssler (Tübinger Beiträge zur Musikwissenschaft, 7)
Whittall, A., 1999:	*Musical Composition in the Twentieth Century*, Oxford, OUP
—, 2003:	*Exploring Twentieth-Century Music*, Cambridge, CUP

ATONAL COMPOSING-OUT

Joseph N. Straus

A central problem in atonal composition (and atonal theory) has to do with organizing and describing relatively large spans of music in coherent ways. One common solution has involved projecting the motives of the musical surface into the deeper levels of structure, deploying them over significant time spans. This musical procedure can be realized in a variety of ways, and has been called historically by a variety of names, including composing-out, concealed repetition, motivic parallelism, nesting, augmentation (enlargement), and self-similarity.[1] In what follows, I will describe and illustrate eight ways of composing-out motives in atonal music.

1. POSITION IN A PHRASE.
A succession of notes or intervals is composed-out as a series of phrase beginnings or endings.

Example 1 contains the opening of the third movement of Ruth Crawford Seeger's *Diaphonic Suite No. 1*.[2] Seeger was an important American composer active mainly in the 1920's and 1930's, and this work was one of a group of four Diaphonic Suites, written as compositional etudes. She described this movement as a "triple passacaglia," which refers to the projection of a basic seven-note series at three different levels of structure.

---

1. There is a vast literature on this subject. The classic discussion from a Schenkerian point of view is Charles Burkhart, "Schenker's 'Motivic Parallelisms'", in: Journal of Music Theory 22 (1978), pp. 145-75. For a more recent account that considers both tonal and atonal repertoire, see Brian Alegant and Donald McLean, "On the Nature of Enlargement", in: *Journal of Music Theory* 45/1 (2001), pp. 31-72.
2. For more extended discussions of this piece and of Seeger's music generally, see Joseph N. Straus, *The Music of Ruth Crawford Seeger*, Cambridge, Cambridge University Press, 1995, and Judith Tick, *Ruth Crawford Seeger: A Composer's Search for American Music*, New York, Oxford University Press, 1997.

Example 1 - Ruth Crawford Seeger, Diaphonic Suite No. 1 (for solo flute or oboe), third movement, mm. 1-20

In measure 1, we see a series: G-A-G#-B-C-F-C#. In measure 2, this series is rotated to begin on its second note. A complete series of rotations follows, culminating in a repeat of the original series in measure 8. The rotational scheme is emphasized by the accents that mark the downbeat of each measure. These accented notes state again, in order, the notes of the series. So we are thus hearing the series at two levels: from eighth-note to eighth-note within each measure and from downbeat to downbeat.

And there is a third level also. In measure 9, the second section of the piece begins with the series transposed up two semitones — now it begins on A, which was the second note of the series at its original level of transposition. This new, transposed form of the series is then systematically rotated, just as the original series was. In measure 18, the third section of the piece is based on a new series form that begins on Ab, the third note of the original series. The notes that begin each section of the piece are shown in boxes in Example 1, and they project the series at a high level of structure. This three-level design shapes the entire movement.

Something similar, although far less systematic, happens in the melodic line of Webern's Song, Op. 3, No. 1. The first four notes of the melody are D-Db-Eb-Gb. The same notes, in the same order, are composed-out as the first notes of the four vocal phrases — see

Example 2 - Webern, Song, Op. 3, No. 1 ("Dies ist ein Lied")

Example 2A. This is about as clear an example of motivic enlargement and motivic nesting as one might wish for.

A somewhat more subtle kind of nesting involves the last four notes of the first phrase: F-Ab-E-Bb. These return, reordered and transposed at the tritone, in the last notes of the four vocal phrases — see Example 2B. The boundary notes at the beginning and ends of phrases thus have the potential to compose-out the notes and intervals of the musical surface.[3]

The same principle is at work over a much larger span of music in the first movement of Schoenberg's Piano Concerto. Schoenberg is working here, as in all of his mature, twelve-tone music, with what are known as "twelve-tone areas". The forty-eight series forms are divided into twelve distinct areas each containing four series forms. The four series within an area are a prime ordering (P), and inversion (I) that contains the same unordered hexachords in reverse order, and the retrogrades of each

---

[3]. For related discussions of this piece, see Robert Wason, "A Pitch-class Motive in Webern's George Lieder, Op. 3", in: Kathryn Bailey (ed.), *Webern Studies*, Cambridge: Cambridge University Press, 1996, pp. 111–34 and Brian Alegant and Donald McLean, "On the Nature of Enlargement."

Joseph N. Straus

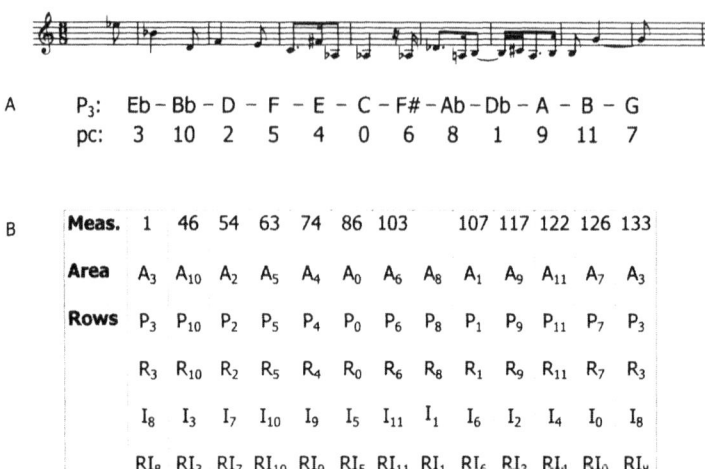

of these (R and RI). In Example 3A, the notes of the original, P-form of the series are identified with pitch-class integers: 3-10-2-5-4-0-6-8-1-9-11-7. As shown in Example 3B, the succession of twelve-tone areas that articulate the harmonic structure of the movement as a whole follows the same pattern: first A3 (which contains P3); then A10 (which contains P10); and so on. This is motivic enlargement on a truly monumental scale.[4]

2. CONTOUR POSITION.
A succession of notes or intervals is composed-out from contour highpoint to highpoint.

Example 4 contains the score for a song by Alban Berg, his Op. 2, No. 2.

Beginning in measure 9, the vocal line describes an attractive shape in which ascending and descending motion are balanced.

---

[4]. For related discussions of this piece, see William Rothstein, "Linear Structure in the Twelve-Tone System: An Analysis of Donald Martino's Pianississimo", in: *Journal of Music Theory* 24 (1980), pp. 129–65 and Andrew Mead, "Twelve-Tone Organizational Strategies: An Analytical Sampler", in: *Integral* 3 (1989), pp. 93–169.

Atonal Composing-Out

Example 4 · Berg, Songs, Op. 2, No. 2

The melody departs from a high Fb. Its next contour highpoint is the Eb in measure 11 and then, preceded by a brief, anacrustic Db, the C on the downbeat of measure 15. These three contour highpoints, Fb-Eb-C, compose-out the first three melodic notes of measure 9, and the same succession is repeated in the piano accompaniment in measure 15. Looking back to the beginning of the song, we see the same succession in the piano in measure 1, and a reordered, transposed version of it in the first three notes of the vocal melody: Cb-G-Bb.

Example 5 - Schoenberg, Piano Piece, Op. 11, No. 1

The frequently analyzed melody from Schoenberg's Op. 11, No. 1 — shown in Example 5 — has a similar design. The melody is in three distinct phrases. In the first phrase (mm. 1-3), the melody descends from a high B. In the second phrase (mm. 4-8), a small fragment reaches up three times to G. In the third phrase (mm. 9-11), a melodic highpoint is attained, briefly but strikingly, on G#. Those three contour highpoints — B-G-G# — compose-out (and slightly reorder) the first three notes of the initial melody. Furthermore, each of the contour highpoints is heard as part of a local statement of the same three-note motive (in its original form or transposed or inverted).[5]

3. REGISTER.
A succession of notes or intervals is composed-out within a single registral line, often the bass.

The eleventh song from Schoenberg's *Book of the Hanging Gardens* begins with a four-note melody: Bb-Db-F-D (see Example 6). Beginning in measure 2, a sustained F in the bass moves first down to D and then, in measure 4, to Db. The Db is embellished with neighbor notes (first C-natural and then Cb), and then sustained

---

5. Example 5 includes an additional large-scale form of the motive projected in the bass, but I will not discuss it here.

Atonal Composing-Out

Example 6 - Schoenberg, Book of the Hanging Gardens, Op. 15, No. 11

(and respelled as C#) through measure 10, where the same three notes are repeated in quick succession. Only one note is needed to create a complete, large-scale statement of the opening four-note melody, and the missing note, Bb, arrives prominently at the end of measure 12, followed immediately by a small-scale restatement of the opening melodic idea. The passage as a whole has an attractive design: a four-note melody is slowly composed out (with changes in register and order) in the bass. At the moment the composing-out is complete, the four-note melody returns in its original order and contour, but now in the bass.⁶

The first movement of Stravinsky's *Serenade in A* begins as in Example 7. A melodic motive, A-Bb-A, is heard repeatedly in the upper voice, over repeated A's in the bass. When the first phrase is over, its end punctuated by the long silence in measure 6, the same motive is transposed down an octave and reharmonized. The new harmonization involves arpeggiations of a Bb-major triad. When this contrasting music peters out into the long silence at the end of measure 14, the opening music returns, reestablishing A as the principal bass note. Stravinsky's compositional sketches for this passage show clearly that the repetition of the opening music was decided upon relatively late in the compositional process, and I hope it is not too fanciful to imagine that Stravinsky did it precisely

Example 7 - Stravinsky, Serenade in A, first movement, mm. 1-20

---

6. My discussion of this song is heavily indebted to David Lewin, "Toward the Analysis of a Schoenberg Song (Op. 15, No. 11)", in: *Perspectives of New Music* 12/1-2 (1973-74), pp. 43-86.

Example 8 - Stravinsky, Septet, first movement, overview

because it produced a large-scale statement of the A-Bb-A motive. Another decision made late in the compositional process was to add the sixteenth-note figuration in measures 1, 3, 4 and elsewhere — in previous sketches the texture was entirely chordal and chorale-like. Notice that embedded within the rapid figuration is yet another statement of A-Bb-A.

In the first movement of Stravinsky's Septet, the bass line that spans the entire movement composes out the initial melodic motive: A-E-D-C-B-A — see Example 8. After the initial fanfare, centered on A, the music shifts abruptly to a kind of E-minor at Rehearsal No. 1. There is an equally sharp break before the music at Rehearsal No. 3, which is centered on D. Then, after a densely canonic passage which is not included in Example 8, the first half of the piece concludes with loud, violent chords with C# in the bass. At this point, having traversed the first four notes of the initial melody (with C# substituting for C), there is a structural interruption and the opening fanfare returns — this is at Rehearsal No. 9. At Rehearsal No. 10, the E-minorish music returns, but only for one measure. It is immediately transposed down a step to D, where it remains. At Rehearsal No. 12, we continue down to C (this is the music that was heard on D in the first half) and then B. Finally, we come to a coda centered on A. Here the opening motives are heard as though recalled from a great distance. The large-scale bass progression, spanning the entire movement, trav0erses the series first partially and then completely. As the bass arrives on its final A, in the coda, the clarinet restates the melody in exactly the same way: first partially and then completely.

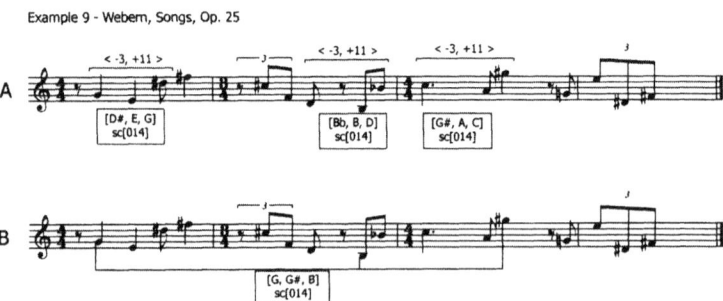

Example 9 - Webern, Songs, Op. 25

4. MELODIC FRAME.
A succession of notes or intervals is composed-out within a melodic frame comprised of the first, last, highest, and lowest notes.

The melody by Webern shown in Example 9A begins with the three-note motive G-E-D#, descending three semitones and then ascending eleven semitones. The same intervallic idea is repeated twice more in the melody, once five semitones lower, D-B-Bb, and once five semitones higher, C-A-G#. Of these three motivic statements, the first note of the first statement, G, is also the first note of the melody; the second note of the second statement, B, is also the lowest note of the melody; and the third note of the third statement, G#, is also the highest note of the melody. The framing motive — G (first), B (lowest), and G# (highest) — is related by transposition (allowing for reordering and octave displacement) to each of the surface motives (see Example 9B).

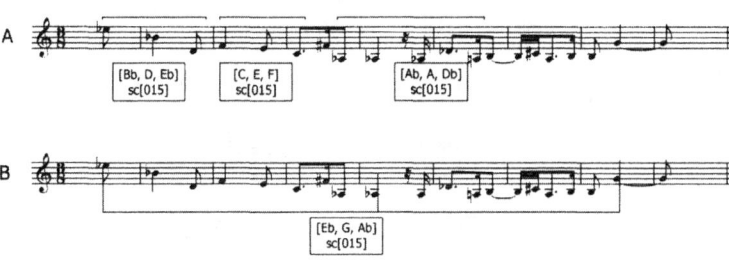

The melody by Schoenberg shown in Example 10A is organized in a similar way. The first three notes, Eb-Bb-D, are transposed onto F-E-C and inverted onto Ab-Db-A (as usual, allowing for reording and octave displacement). A larger melodic frame composed of the first and highest note (Eb), the lowest note (Ab), and the last note (G) is related to these by either transposition or inversion (see Example 10B).

5. DYNAMICS.
A succession of notes or intervals is composed-out within a single shared dynamic level.

Within a musical texture, notes may be associated with each other in a variety of ways, through shared timbre, register, dynamic level, or any other musical quality. More formally, we might say that notes can form meaningful musical associations if they share

Example 11 - Milton Babbitt, String Quartet No. 2

mp:	A-C-Ab	<+3,-4>	p:	D-Gb-Eb	<+4,-3>
pp:	B-D-Bb	<+3,-4>	fff:	E-Ab-F	<+4,-3>
ff:	F-C#-E	<-4,+3>	ppp:	Bb-G-B	<-3,+4>
mf:	G-Eb-Gb	<-4,+3>	f:	C-A-Db	<-3,+4>

Atonal Composing-Out

a value in some domain (i.e. they are high, or low, or loud, or soft).[7] And once notes are associated in this way, the interval formed between them has motivic potential. Babbitt's String Quartet No. 2 (and a lot of his other music) realizes that potential in a systematic way — see Example 11.

In measures 1–3, we hear six melodic statements of a single interval, +3 (or its inverse, -9, or its compound, +15). In measures 4–6, we hear eight statements of another interval, -4 (or its inverse, +8). Beginning in measure 7, these two intervals are combined into a single three-note motive that undergoes intensive, systematic development. In measure 7, for example, reading down through the score we hear four different combinations of 3 and 4: <+3, -4> in the first violin; <-4, +3> in the second violin; <-3, +4> in the viola; and <+4, -3> in the cello. In measures 7–12, the same thing happens within each instrumental line: four statements of a three-note motive that combines a 3 and a 4 moving in opposite directions.

Looking back at measures 1–3 and 4–6, we find the same three-note motive projected within each of eight dynamic levels. The notes marked *mp*, for example, are A-C-Ab, representing the intervallic succession <+3, -4>. This exact succession of notes, projected here within a shared dynamic level, returns in measure 7 as a direct statement by the first violin. Notes that are associated by virtue of a shared dynamic level thus project in this more concealed way the motivic concerns of the musical surface.[8]

6. DURATION.
A succession of notes or intervals is composed-out through shared durational values.

What Babbitt does with shared dynamic levels, Stravinsky does with shared durational values. The song "Music to hear," the first of

---

7. I am adopting the terminology of Christopher Hasty, "Segmentation and Process in Post-Tonal Music", in: *Music Theory Spectrum* 3 (1981), pp. 54–73.
8. For a more extended discussion of this passage, see Joseph N. Straus, "Listening to Babbitt", in: *Perspectives of New Music* 25 (1987), pp. 3–24. For discussion of Babbitt's music generally, including his use of dynamics to present serial ideas, see Andrew Mead, *The Music of Milton Babbitt*, Princeton, Princeton University Press, 1994.

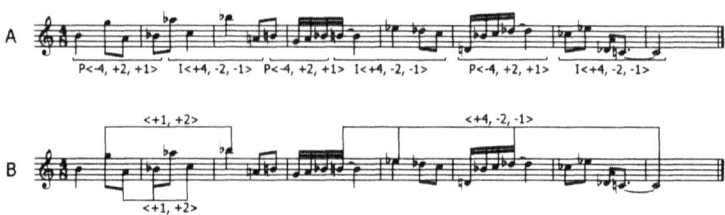

Example 12 - Stravinsky, Three Shakespeare Songs ("Musick to heare"), opening flute melody

the *Three Shakespeare Songs*, is based on a four-note series: B-G-A-Bb. Example 12A offers a serial analysis of the opening flute melody, which alternates prime and inverted statements of the series.

Beginning in measure 4, the second of the inverted statements involves the succession B-Eb-Db-C. As shown in Example 12B, beginning at the same place in the melody, the longest durational values compose-out the same succession of notes. In this way, Stravinsky projects a series statement over a relatively longer span of music, by associating notes that share a durational value. Example 12B also shows the use of register for the same purpose: in the first two measures, the highest and lowest registral lines both project series subsets.

7. TIMBRE (INSTRUMENTATION).
A succession of notes or intervals is composed-out through shared timbre.

Like dynamics and duration, timbre can be used to associate notes that are separated in time, and the thus-associated notes may project significant intervals or motives. Webern's Concerto for nine instruments, Op. 24, is a twelve-tone piece, and the four trichords of its series are all of the same type, members of set-class (014). Example 13A contains the first eleven measures of the second movement, comprising three complete statements of the series and the beginning of a fourth. The trichords contained in each of the series are circled on the example.

Over the course of the music, Webern finds a variety of ways of projecting the same motive-type over larger musical spans. The music is divided clearly into a melody (shared by eight melodic

Atonal Composing-Out

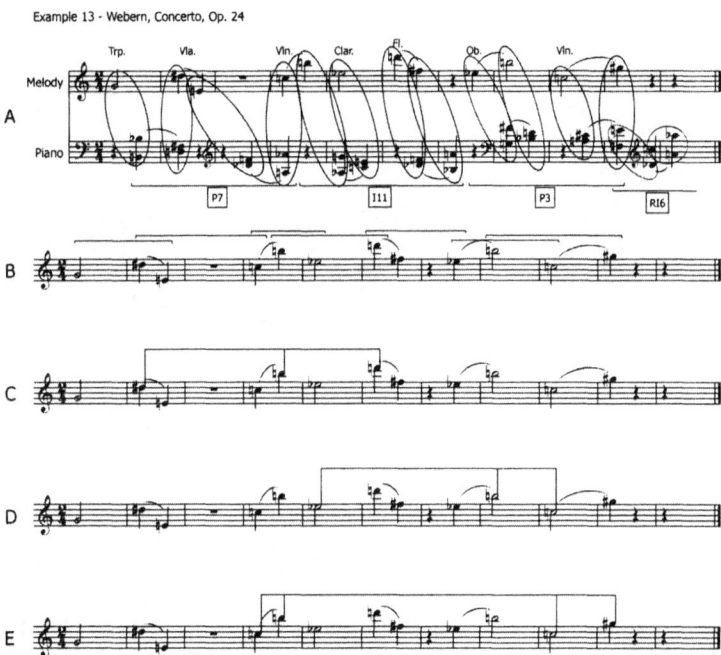

Example 13 - Webern, Concerto, Op. 24

instruments) and an accompaniment in the piano, which plays continuously. The shared melodic line, which cuts across the series and its trichords, nonetheless also projects forms of (014) — these are bracketed on Example 13B. Within the melodic line, the contour highpoints also project a form of (014) — see Example 13C — while the longer durational values project another — see Example 13D. Finally, Example 13E isolates the three notes played by the violin: like the projections through contour and duration, these timbrally associated notes also project a form of (014). In this way, the persistent motive of the musical surface is also composed-out, in an amazing variety of ways, over larger musical spans.

8. TRANSPOSITIONAL PROJECTION.
A motive is composed-out by being projected along a transpositional path.

A particularly rich compositional resource involves what I call "transpositional projection". A musical motive is transposed by

Joseph N. Straus

Example 14 - Webern, Movement for String Quartet, Op. 5, No. 2

B (G) — T4 → (B)   (G) — T6 → (C#)
       same

C (Eb G A) — T4 → (G B C#)   (C# F G) — T6 → (G B C#)
                      same

intervals it contains. Intervals thus are projected at two levels: within the motive and between the transposed forms of the motive. It is often convenient to represent relationships of this kind as networks modeled by graphs consisting of nodes and arrows, and that is what I will do in the musical examples that follow.

Example 14 contains the opening of the second of Webern's Five Movements for string quartet, Op. 5. The passage is organized as a lyrical melody in the viola accompanied by chords in the second violin and cello. The initial melodic motive in the viola consists of four notes: G-B-G-C#. We can think of that as in Example 14B as two transpositional gestures, first T4 taking us from G to B and then T6 taking us from G to C#. Both gestures depart from the same note, the G.

Looking now at the accompanying chords, we notice that the final chord has the same notes as the viola's melodic motive: G, B, and C#. The chord that immediately precedes it moves to the final chord by T4, thus replicating the viola's initial melodic gesture. And there is an additional three-note motive embedded in the viola melody that also can be heard to transpose onto the final chord, by T6, replicating the viola's second melodic gesture. Both of these gestures arrive at the same place, the trichord [G, B, C#]. These relationships are summarized in Example 14C. The same musical gestures that take us from note to note in the initial

Atonal Composing-Out

Example 15 - Schoenberg, Book of the Hanging Gardens, Op. 15, No. 11

[musical score]

motive thus also take us from harmony to harmony in the concluding progression.[9]

Example 15 takes another look at a passage we discussed previously, the opening of the eleventh song from Schoenberg's *Book of*

---

9. For a related discussion of this passage, see David Lewin, "Transformational Techniques in Atonal and Other Music Theories", in: *Perspectives of New Music* 21 (1982–83), pp. 312–371.

the Hanging Gardens, Op. 15.[10] The song begins with a four-note piano motive that can be described as taking a single note, the Bb, and transposing it successively by T3 and then T4 (Example 15B). If we now consider the motive as a whole, we can chart its progress over the course of the passage. Confining our attention to the alto register in which it is first presented, we find two statements of the same gesture, T3 followed by T4 (Example 15C). The three networks of Example 15, the first referring to a succession of notes, the second and third to a succession of motives, can thus be represented by the same graph. We would say that these three networks

---

10. The following discussion draws heavily upon David Lewin, "Toward the Analysis of a Schoenberg Song (Op. 15, No. 11)".

are "isographic".[11] In other words, the same musical gesture that defines the note-to-note succession within the motive is also composed-out, at a higher level of structure, in the harmony-to-harmony succession of the larger musical spans.

In Stravinsky's music, the spans involved can be truly monumental, reaching from the beginning of a work to its end. Example 16A shows the beginning of *Les Noces* and identifies intervals in the melody: a plus-2 from D to E, a minus-5 from E to B, and a resulting minus-3 from D to B.

The same fragment occurs at many transposition levels during the work, but most insistently and often as in Example 16B, which is the beginning of the third scene. The motive has now been transposed two semitones higher. The work concludes with one of those remarkable, protracted Stravinskian codas, where time seems to stop amid slow, obsessive repetition of a small melodic fragment. Example 16C contains a small bit of the coda, and the melodic fragment consists of G#-B-C#, now 3 semitones below the work's opening in Example 16A and 5 semitones below the beginning of the third scene in Example 16B. The motive has been transposed by the intervals it contains. The resulting large-scale progression, one that spans the entire work, thus replicates the intervallic shape of the original motive.

Example 17A reproduces the vocal melody from the *Lacrimosa* movement of Stravinsky's last major work, the *Requiem Canticles*. The analytical markings indicate that this melody is embedded in a structure that comes from the array in Example 17B. All of Stravinsky's major twelve-tone pieces during the last phase of his compositional life are based on arrays like this one.

In arrays of this type, one of the hexachords of a twelve-note series is written across the top row (labeled with Roman Numeral I). To get from the first row to the second, you simultaneously rotate and transpose. In this case, D (which is the second note of the first row) simultaneously moves into the first position in the second row and moves up 5 semitones to G. The E, which was the

---

11. The use of networks and graphs is characteristic of "transformational theory", the principal contribution of David Lewin. See, among many other sources, his *Generalized Musical Intervals and Transformations*, New Haven, Yale University Press, 1987.

Example 17 - Stravinsky, Requiem Canticles ("Lacrimosa")

third note in the first row, moves into the second position in the second row, and moves up 5 semitones to A. The F, which was the fourth note in the first row, moves into the third position in the second row, and moves up 5 semitones to A#. So each note in the first row moves one position to the left and up five semitones.

Why do you have to transpose 5 semitones to get from the first row to the second? The answer has to do with the interval between the first two notes in the first row: G and D. From G to D you go down 5 semitones, so to get from the D in the first row to the G at the beginning of the second you have to go up 5 semitones. The interval between the first two rows is the reverse of the interval between the first two notes in the first row.

In moving from the second row to the third row, the same thing happens, only now the interval of transposition is 10, not 5. The second note of the second row, A, moves up 10 semitones and one position to the left to become the first note of the third row, G. That interval of transposition (10) is the reverse of the interval (2) between the second and third notes, the D and the E. Stravinsky always chooses transpositions that will keep the G as the first note of every row. So all of the rows of the array are related by transposition, and the sequence of transpositions mirrors the intervals of the row itself.

The Lacrimosa melody in Example 17A is based directly on the array. The first melodic phrase is the sixth row of the array sung in retrograde order. The second melodic phrase is the fifth row of the array in prime order. The third melodic phrase is the fourth and third rows of the array and the last melodic phrase is the second and first rows of the array. The melody as a whole, then, cycles through the array systematically from bottom to top. I have indicated the transpositions that take us from phrase to phrase: T2-T8-T1-T2-T7.

Compare these transpositional intervals with the melodic intervals within each phrase, for example within the last melodic phrase, which corresponds to the first row of the array. There, we hear the same intervals, in reverse order, as the transpositions that connected the melodic hexachords. We thus hear a certain sequence of intervals within the hexachord, and the same sequence of intervals between the hexachords. In short, the motive is transposed by the intervals it contains.

Stravinsky liked these special arrays, because they offered him a systematic way of reenacting a familiar compositional procedure, namely to transpose the motive by the intervals it contains. Arrays like the one in Example 17B are designed to hardwire that possibility. Now, the intervals *within* the rows return, at a higher level, as the intervals of transposition *between* the rows. And when Stravinsky's late melodies move systematically through the array, like the melody in Example 17A and so many of his melodies, that principle becomes the audible basis for joining the musical moments into larger shapes.

SYSTEMLESSNESS IN MUSIC

Composing Without a System:
a Comparative Study of Systemlessness
in the Works of John Cage, Morton Feldman
and Wolfgang Rihm

Yves Knockaert

INTRODUCTION

Only at certain stages of their development did Cage, Feldman and Rihm work without a system. The present paper analyzes those stages in order to find out why those composers decided to work that way, and what the consequences of that decision were for their aesthetic considerations in music.

At first sight, composing without relying on a system, or method, looks a daunting, or even impossible, task. The composer is indeed bereft of any reference that might help him shape and develop his creation, direct it, or construct and deconstruct it. The notion of systemlessness usually evokes a feeling of disorder, chaos and anarchy, while musicologists too are at pains to come to grips with the asystematic. Music without a system is hard to analyze. The result of such an analysis can never be complete, let alone satisfactory, while the study of works based on one system or another (repetitive, serial etc.) can. That explains the absence of thorough analyses of systemless compositions. In 1996, Thomas DeLio wrote this in his introduction to *The Music of Morton Feldman* (a compilation of several analyses): "At present (...) there exist few serious scholarly studies of his work".[1] In 2002, at the occasion of his fiftieth birthday, Rihm answered one remark with respect to the relatively small number of scholarly studies given the number of works he had written by saying that such studies would soon appear. The

---

1. DeLio, *The Music of Morton Feldman*, p. XIII.

next question was: "So is my impression wrong that musical scholars are unhappy with the difficulty of coming to grips with your music?" Rihm: "I believe this has more to do with the fact that, from the onset, I have been striving for works of art that cannot be analyzed. That is a challenge I discovered in Claude Debussy's approach, and decided to make part of my own world. I have no desire to supplement what I write with any form of analysis whatsoever."[2] When trying to analyze systemless works, one also needs to ask oneself whether such creations can be analyzed at all.

Even Cage's random compositions have only been described, but never really analyzed. In his *Indeterminacy* lecture (1958), Cage admitted that in Feldman he had a predecessor with respect to the degree of indeterminacy, which is akin to systemlessness. He made a clear distinction between the indeterminate dimension of composing and performing music, and explained the difference between his approach and Feldman's:

> This is a lecture on composition which is indeterminate with respect to its performance. The 'Intersection 3' by Morton Feldman is an example. The 'Music of Changes' is not an example.
> In the 'Music of Changes',
> structure, which is the division of the whole into parts;
> method, which is the note-to-note procedure;
> form, which is the expressive content, the morphology of the continuity;
> and materials, the sounds and silences of the composition,
> are all determined.
> In the case of the 'Intersection 3' by Morton Feldman,
> structure may be viewed as determinate or as indeterminate;
> method is definitely indeterminate.
> Frequency and duration characteristics of the material are determinate only within broad limits (they are with respect to narrow limits indeterminate);
> the timbre characteristics of the material, being given by the instrument designated, the piano, is determinate;

---

2. Fricke, "Musik ist nie bei sich", in: *NZfM* (2002), 2, p. 53.

The amplitude characteristics of the material is indeterminate.
Form conceived in terms of a continuity of various weights — that is, a continuity of numbers of sounds, the sounds themselves particularized only with respect to broad range limits (high, middle, and low) — is determinate, particularly so due to the composer's having specified boxes as time units. Though one might equally describe it as indeterminate for other reasons. (...)
With the exception of method, which is wholly indeterminate, the compositional means are characterized by being in certain respects determinate, in others indeterminate, and an interpenetration of these opposites obtains which is more characteristic than either. The situation is therefore essentially non-dualistic; a multiplicity of centers in a state of non-obstruction and interpenetration.[3]

1. JOHN CAGE
1.1. NON-INTENTION:
SYSTEMATIC AND SYSTEMLESS AT THE SAME TIME

Strictly speaking, Cage has never worked without a compositional system. Non-intention, the desire to work with random possibilities, was his system. He had reached that stage by first declaring that his personal taste, his subjective and individual interventions and judgements should not interfere with his work. He saw the severe limitations of individual interventions by the composer: such a person is unable to transcend himself and to contemplate other possibilities than his own. Personal taste is therefore a restriction of the infinite number of possibilities, a restriction of freedom. By calling this a "restriction", I also suggest that the "style" concept constitutes a limiting factor: it can indeed be defined as a series of recurring figures, development strategies and processes that set a composer apart from all others and thus make him recognizable. Ultimately, I can therefore claim that the absence of style, based on indeterminacy, necessarily leads to total freedom and therefore to absolute creativity. Cage, for his part, did not adopt indeterminacy right away, though. He discovered the

---

3. Cage, "Composition as Process, II. Indeterminacy", in: *Silence*, p. 36.

liberation of self-restriction in a compositional method based on the "I Jing", a method or systematic approach that allowed him to use non-intention in an organized way. From the point of view of non-intention as underlying system, the various stages he went through during the four decades since the 1950s can be summarized as follows: Cage analyzed a maximum number of possibilities of organized non-intention. He left the sequence of musical figures to the performers by devising random scores of fixed material (thus preserving a set of musical figures). Later, he indicated the pitch and duration of the notes on his graphic scores. That finally led him to a point where he merely provided the "input" for a musical or non-musical happening: his work consisted of bringing a bunch of people together, both musicians and non-musicians, inviting them to take part in the event. It goes without saying that the non-musicians' input was usually also non-music. It also goes without saying that Cage, having reached that stage, no longer used any compositional system whatsoever, the reason being that he had taken to collecting possibilities rather composing proper. Sometimes, he remained in control of an event by operating the mixing console, or because he used the "I Jing" for specifying its duration. In other cases, however, nothing was set beforehand, not even the duration, and Cage had no influence whatsoever on the event. His part was therefore restricted to one of instigator, the person that suggests the concept. The most important stages of the aforesaid evolution were: *Music of Changes* (1950s), the *Variations* series, and *0'00"* in the 1960s. *Musicircus* and other similar concepts were developed in the 1960s and 1970s, and finally there was the *Number Pieces* series created in his last years. Throughout those various stages, Cage analyzed non-intention in all its aspects. The most dramatic non-intentional compositions and projects were created before the early 1970s, after which he failed to reach meaningful new insights. In a way, the *Number Pieces* are only a strict application of a limited number of random possibilities from a rather more harmonic and consonant point of view than what he had done until then.

The "I Jing" was essential for Cage's elaboration of non-intention. "I Jing" can be defined in a paradoxical way by calling it a compositional system without a system, or an asystematic way of composing. Both definitions contain the same contradiction in terms: the presence and absence of a system, or method. The actual meaning is that the "I Jing" provides the possibility to devise musical scores without any other method apart from that of indeterminacy. Random operations not only guarantee the complete absence of the composer's personal taste, but also his acceptance of the infinite number of unrestricted possibilities. That infinity is only restricted by the rules Cage himself imposes on coincidence (and this is precisely where the contradiction is solved: here, the asystematic nature of indeterminacy is subjected to a directive system). Cage indeed devised a new set of "I Jing" rules for every new composition; the limits of such a set of rules and the number of combinations they provide determined the limits, thus constituting a restriction of total and utter freedom of indeterminacy. Here is an example: if you start out by deciding that 80% of the possibilities shall be silence, while the remaining 20% shall be sounds, it is relatively certain (according to the Gauss curve) that the "I Jing" will randomly produce about 80% of silence in the final composition. That, however, is only one possibility, it is an "average" if you will, which is a far cry from reality. Indeterminacy may indeed lead to 100% of silence or 100% of sound. One thing is certain however: you can never obtain other results than those allowed by the set of rules (that "shape" indeterminacy) you have decided to work with. Probability and unpredictability go hand in hand and may lead to a degree of serendipity, the discovery of totally unexpected possibilities, that, at least as far as Cage is concerned, are equally unintended.

Yet, we all know that chance is merely a virtual concept, a pre-existence that constitutes an open possibility. Chance exists, and its six possibilities are equally likely, until you roll the dice. After throwing them, however, when the dice stop rolling, total indeterminacy of the dice's six possibilities vanishes and is replaced by the limitation of a single result. As far as I'm concerned, that is not a breaking point, not even a problem, because it is inherently related to chance and to the final decision related to the use of probability. One always ends up with a single possibility among an infinite number of possibilities. What I do not accept as such, however, is the difference between a decision I take, without any obligation, regarding e.g. the duration of a composition, and the fact that the duration should be determined by random operations. In the first case, it is safe to say that the duration was determined without relying on a given system; in the second case, the random operations constitute a system that determines the duration. I therefore need to keep considering the use of the "I Jing" a system. I could stop right here and conclude that indeterminate or systemless composition has nothing to do with Cage's music. A different conclusion is, however, equally possible: save for the choice one makes, the "I Jing's" random system is utterly indeterminate, unpredictable. All possibilities are and remain equally likely. In that respect, the use of random possibilities for composing music inherently contains systemlessness, because it is indeterminacy that decides, and because one needs to take decisions with respect to chance based on coincidence as a method. Indeterminacy is thus guaranteed in two ways, thereby allowing us to analyze how Cage devised this asystematic way of composing.

1.2. STRUCTURE, METHOD, MATERIAL

In my introduction, I already cited the definitions that Cage had provided for the terms "structure", "method" and "form". According to those definitions, "structure" is "the division of the whole into parts". Initially, Cage himself used fractions for specifying the relationship between a composition's parts and the whole. Later on, he left that decision to the "I Jing", which was also solicited for specifying the duration of a composition. After that, the structure only emerged at the time of implementation of a piece by means of a graphic score, without any preconceived structure. To these possibilities elaborated by Cage, one might also add improvisation and random principles, where a structure only materializes at the time of writing. Regardless of the specific case one contemplates, I believe that the structure is always determined by the sound being composed or performed (if it wasn't composed beforehand). This leads us to the following two considerations: if Cage saw his structure only as a relationship of predefined durations, the structure has an abstract nature and is therefore an empty framework rather than an actual musical structure. The actual musical structure only emerges once the empty framework is filled with sound. In that respect, improvisation represents an equally empty structure whose shape becomes apprehendable once it is filled with sound. The sounds and the relationships between those sounds create the actual structure.

Whenever one defines sounds by writing them down in a composition (regardless of whether they are chosen deliberately or ad random), or by performing them, one immediately imposes a structure, or at least the starting point for a structure. One starts with the creation of a structure, thus making it impossible to escape from it. Consequently, a structure can never exist without a system (whether predefined or emerging on the spot), which is why a structure can never be non-intended. Even for his "Tacet" piece, *4'33"*, Cage was only interested in one thing — a structure which he had divided into three parts for the occasion, each part having a structured duration: 30", 2'23" and 1'40". Less is impossible, even though one of the consequences of *4'33"* is that the listener can declare anything they hear during this piece to be music. At one stage, he or she will decide to start listening, and later to stop listening again. In that respect, the listener defines the beginning and end of his or her composition, or structure. The listener chooses the structure or framework of that composition, using the sounds he or she hears "by accident" to fill that structure. Scientific minds fond of extremes might say that even an infinite musical piece has a structure: there is a beginning, because it was necessarily started by someone, while eternity is also a structuring standard in that one knows that the piece will never end. At the other end of the longest piece is the shortest: that one inaudible structure of music is as definite as all other structures. I am referring to a piece consisting of a single sound that is too short to be perceived by the human ear. It may not exist for human perception, yet it is there, and clearly structured with the intention to conceal its existence. That inaudible piece of music is therefore subject to strict systemic rules, i.e. the laws of perception by the human ear, which are related to the limitation of human beings.

Thus, a structure is always defined and therefore necessarily subject to a system. Even if the composer did not present the system on purpose, it is nevertheless there in its implementation. The easiest way to define that system is by saying that it is based on the phenomenon of comparison. The listener compares consecutive or simultaneous sounds with one another and determines how they differ in pitch, duration and other aspects. Cage's "method" and "material" concepts are an altogether different matter. A method, to Cage, is a "note-to-note procedure", while the material is defined as "the sounds and silences of the composition". Composing in a traditional sense means that one creates functionality, a relationship between the sounds, both horizontally and vertically. The composer forces the sounds in a given direction, the result of this intention being a "composition" in the literal sense of the word, i.e. a compound of notes. Even the term "musical piece" hints at related sounds, otherwise we would have to call each musical product "musical pieces", i.e. in the plural form. Whenever Cage uses the "I Jing" as method or system, his material is free of intentions, while the method is "system-free", as I showed in the ostensible contradiction above.

1.3. FROM MUSIC OF CHANGES TO $0'00''$

It is interesting to see how the terminology Cage uses to describe the traditionally scored *Sonatas and Interludes* already contains references to the non-intentional approach he was to adopt much later. (For the sake of completeness: that description was written in 1958, when Cage's non-intentional ideas were maturing; it is thus ten years younger than *Sonatas and Interludes*).

"In the case of the 'Sonatas and Interludes', only structure was organized, quite roughly for the work as a whole, exactly, however, within each single piece. The method was that of considered improvisation, mainly at the piano, though ideas came to me at some moments away from the instrument. The materials, the piano preparations, were chosen as one chooses shells walking along a beach."[4] Chance is already lurking around the corner:

---

4. Cage, "Composition as Process, I. Changes", in: *Silence*, p. 19.

Cage mentions improvisation, and he uses the analogy of shells on the beach, which are there in high numbers. Choosing one among them may still be governed by personal taste, yet the sheer number of shells, the coincidental or random nature of such a choice, i.e. the asystematic, plays a certain part here. Looking at all the shells before picking one, or several, is virtually impossible. And even though Cage talks about improvisation, the structure of *Sonatas and Interludes* is very strict indeed: he uses a lot of literal repetitions and variations of short motifs. His understanding of musical structure is strikingly traditional. This composition is an illustration of Cage's awareness of his own limitation, and hence of his "style". He knew exactly what he wanted to get away from. *Music of Changes* (1951) does not question the determination of structure. Cage still works with predefined numeric relationships that determine the duration of the composition's periods. Due to the first implementation of the "I Jing", i.e. the method, the "note-to-note procedure" changes dramatically, yet the compositional approach still controls the structure: "Chance operations determined stability or change of tempo. Thus, by introducing the action of method into the body of the structure, and these two opposed in terms of order and freedom, that structure became indeterminate: it was not possible to know the total time-length of the piece until the final chance operation, the last toss of coins affecting the rate of tempo, had been made. Being indeterminate, though still present, it became apparent that structure was not necessary, even though it had certain uses."[5]

After freeing the structure from predetermination by introducing the concept of variable duration for the parts, Cage can do away with the necessity for a structure as a framework, thus abandoning a structure that acts as "pre-concept". He did so right after *Music of Changes*, in his 84-part *Music for Piano* (1952–56; part 85 "for piano and electronic sound-modifying devices" was only added in 1962): "In *Music for Piano*, and subsequent pieces, structure is indeed no longer a part of the composition means".[6]

---

5. ibid., p. 20–21.
6. ibid., p. 22.

Consequently, even the duration of a composition is no longer pre-determined. This is not only achieved by determining the structure with the "I Jing", but also in a far more dramatic way by adding the possibility of performing several parts of *Music for Piano* simultaneously (the piece can be played by one to twenty pianists). The scope and consistency of the stages of increasing indeterminacy and systemlessness can be inferred from the fact that even the rhythm (the duration of each sound within the composition) is indeterminate: "In *Music for Piano*, structure no longer being present, the piece took place in any length of time whatsoever, according to the exigencies of an occasion. The duration of single sounds was therefore also left indeterminate. The notation took the form of whole notes in space."[7] Thanks to this increasing indeterminacy, the composition changes to process music: "The view taken is not of an activity the purpose of which is to integrate the opposites, but rather of an activity characterized by process and essentially purposeless. The mind, though stripped of its right to control, is still present. What does it do, having nothing to do? And what happens to a piece of music when it is purposelessly made?"[8] Cage believes that purposeless or asystematic music should also influence perception: "A mind (of the listener) that has nothing to do, is free to enter into the act of listening, hearing each sound just as it is, not as a phenomenon more or less approximating a preconception."[9] Even the perception and the choreography of silence are subjected to a fundamental transformation: "Silence becomes something else — not silence at all, but sounds, the ambient sounds. The nature of these is unpredictable and changing."[10] It is hard to overstress the importance of all these transformations for the aesthetics of composition and why they are, in fact, the first steps towards total systemlessness, meaning that nothing is set or put together by a system, i.e. "composed". The sum becomes process music, indeterminate and arising out of chance. In that respect, it is totally and utterly at odds

---

7. ibid., p. 30.
8. ibid., p. 22.
9. ibid., p. 23.
10. ibid., p. 22.

with the classic, system-based way of composing. In his comments on *Music for Piano*, Cage therefore comes to the following conclusion: "Finally, nothing has been determined by the notation as far as performance time is concerned. And, as concerns timbre, next to nothing has been determined. And — and this may be considered a fundamental omission — nothing has been indicated regarding the architecture of the room in which the music is to be played and the placement (customarily distant one from another) of the instruments (how many?) therein. All these elements, evidently of paramount importance, point the question: What has been composed?"[11]

Ill. 1. Cage, Variations V, first page of the score.

```
SOUND-SYSTEM (A) HAVING CONTINUOUSLY OPERATING (TAPE MA-
CHINES (6+), SHORT WAVE RECEIVERS (6+), OSCILLATOR(S) (B) )
AND, OPTIONALLY, NON-CONTINUOUSLY OPERATING (ELECTRON-
IC PERCUSSION DEVICES (B)(6+) SOUND-SOURCES.

AUDIBILITY OF SOUND-SYSTEM DEPENDENT ON MOVEMENT OF
DANCERS (C), THROUGH INTERRUPTION OF LIGHT BEAMS(D)(6+)
PROXIMITY TO ANTENNAS (B) (4+).

PERFORMANCE WITHOUT SCORE OR PARTS.

TELEVISION (PREFERABLY CLOSED WITH IMAGE DISTORTIONS (E))AND/
OR FILM (PREFERABLY MULTIPLE) PROJECTION OF DANCE AND
OTHER IMAGES(F).

VARIATION: PLACEMENT OF PHOTO-ELECTRIC CELLS ON THE IMAGE
SCREEN.

AS THOUGH THERE WERE A DRAWING OF THE CONTROLS AVAIL-
ABLE AND - ON A TRANSPARENCY - TRANSCRIPTION FROM
ASTRONOMICAL ATLAS WHICH (WERE IT SUPERIMPOSED)
WOULD GIVE SUGGESTIONS FOR USE OF CONTROLS.

RELAYS (P) PERMITTING AUDIBILITY OF SOUND-SOURCES TO CON-
TINUE FOR A PERIOD VARIABLE BY DIAL CONTROL FROM 0 TO
2½ MINUTES.


(A) DESIGNED BY DAVID TUDOR.
(B) DEVISED BY ROBERT MOOG.
(C) CHOREOGRAPHY BY MERCE CUNNINGHAM.
(D) PHOTO-ELECTRIC DEVICES DEVISED BY BILLY KLUVER.
(E) DESIGNED BY NAM JUNE PAIK.
(F) FILM BY STAN VANDERBEEK.
```

---

11. Cage, "To Describe the Process of Composition Used in 'Music for Piano 21–52'", in: *Silence*, p. 61.

Ill. 2. Cage, Variations V, 1965 performance. Front (left to right) John Cage, David Tudor and Gordon Mumma. Back: the dancers Merce Cunningham and Barbara Lloyd.

Even though this means I have to stray away from the chronological order of Cage's works, the next stage consists of increasing freedom and systemlessness, as applied in *Variations* (1958–66). Here, the score, i.e. the action plan for the performer, has been replaced by sheets of paper with dots and lines, whose superposition results in a "score", whereby the distance between the lines and dots needs to be interpreted based on the determination of the various characteristics of the sound to be played. Cage manages to work with total freedom and systemlessness: no pre-concept, no control, and no purpose. What's more, even the composition itself is absent, which necessarily means that there is no system whatsoever. Cage even leaves the musical domain by using the term "performer", or "player", and by giving specifically non-musical instructions for certain Variations: "This experience is not only received by the ears but by the eyes too".[12] The same can be inferred from the subtitles and performance instructions provided by Cage:

> Variations III: for one or any number of people performing any actions;
> Variations IV: for any number of players, any sounds or combinations of sounds produced by any means, with or without other activities;

---

12. Cage, "Composition as Process, I. Changes", in: *Silence*, p. 31.

Variations V: 37 remarks re an Audio-Visual Performance;
Variations VI: the notation refers to what is to be done, not to what is heard or to be heard.

The absence of a "composition" as such also leads to works without a beginning, middle part or end, without any subdivisions, etc.: "They begin anywhere, last any length of time, and involve more or fewer instrumentists and players".[13] Another consequence is that he includes the location as a new and totally freely useable element in his compositions, something that Cages explained in his *Indeterminacy* lecture. The important aspect of that lecture is the way in which Cage approaches the time dimension. In his *Lecture on Nothing*, he drew the audience's attention to the fact that he had nothing to say. All he did was helping the audience to experience the lapse of time by regularly stating how long he had been at it. The illustration of the time dimension and the act of breaking it is much stronger still in *Indeterminacy*, which he created one year later. There, Cage uses a pattern that is constantly repeated: he repeats large chunks of text, with minimal variations or alterations, thus doing away with the lapse-of-time notion. After all, he suddenly reaches a "moment" he had already visited before; he literally goes back in time, as it were. By doing so, he once again expresses purposelessness, while at the same time putting the contents of what he is saying into perspective. What is important here are both the realization of time passing and the relativity of time. Moreover, this is a confirmation of his process idea, because literal repetitions are, after all, impossible, no matter how hard a narrator or performer tries.

I think one can link this resolve of the time dimension to an asystematic approach of the time dimension, which, though seemingly impossible in music, is exactly what Cage effectively did. The time and space dimensions are therefore tremendously important in those compositions that have their duration as a title: *4'33"* and *0'00"* (1952 and '62 respectively). During this study of

---

13. ibid.

systemlessness, *o'oo"* (with its subtitle *4'33" no. 2*) is even more important than *4'33"*. Its first total indeterminacy concerns its duration: Cage no longer deems it necessary to set a time limit. Unlike silence, the one element used in *4'33"*, *o'oo"* is a "solo to be performed in any way by anyone", thus, a spatial performance, where anything but what Cage forbids is allowed: the performance of the score of an existing composition. He describes it as follows: "In a situation provided with maximum amplification (no feedback), perform a disciplined action." Thus, in *o'oo"*, nothing has been composed, nothing is limited, an even chance is no longer at work during the performance. The zero duration was chosen arbitrarily, but is therefore the most absolute confirmation of systemlessness and at the same time Cage's first piece one can rightfully call asystematic. There is no score anymore, not even an action plan in the guise of overhead sheets as used for *Variations*, which were, after all, instructions for the implementation. Stronger still than the attitude of a performance, dissociated from music, the very asystematic nature of *o'oo"* is a subjective work of art. As stated earlier, Cage had used his random operations precisely to suppress his personal taste, whereas a performance of *o'oo"* is inevitably subjective. Total systemlessness therefore coincides with the re-emergence of subjectivity. In later works, like *Musicircus*, where Cage invites artists to take part in a joint performance, that same subjectivity is coupled with the highest degree of systemlessness, a "rule-free environment extravaganza": "It simply consisted of inviting people ready to partake to perform together (in the same place and at the same time)".[14] There were musicians and there was music at the première in 1969, yet there were also lots of non-musical elements, like films, slides, balloons...

1.4. STORIES

It strikes one that Cage complements his lectures with made-up stories and anecdotes from his own life. Towards the end of the *Changes* lecture, Cage says: "I have not yet told any stories and yet

---

14. Kostelanetz, *John Cage*, p. 233.

when I give a talk I generally do".[15] And then he starts telling a story, after which he adds: "That was not the story I was going to tell when I first thought I would tell one, but it reminds me of another". So he tells a second story, and then says: "Now I remember the story I was going to tell when I first got the idea to tell one." The question why Cage should be telling stories is far more important than the contents of those stories. Except for the moral, or fundamental, truth of the stories, Cage most certainly does it because art is always related to real life, art is identified with life. By telling a story, Cage talks about his art. Of course, those stories are also illustrations of the part of chance in everyday life, which is why they fit right in with the systemlessness of his art. His stories are, after all, usually very humble and make everybody laugh, including Cage himself. The penultimate chapter of the book *Silence* was again called *Indeterminacy* and consists of a collection of thirty stories that Cage had read during the 1958 World Exhibition in Brussels. The following story is the perfect example of systemlessness no matter what.

> A crowded bus on the point of leaving Manchester for Stockport was found by its conductress to have one too many standees. She therefore asked, "Who was the last person to get on the bus?" No one said a word. Declaring that the bus would not leave until the extra passenger was put off, she went and fetched the driver, who also asked, "All right, who was the last person to get on the bus?" Again there was a public silence. So the two went to find an inspector. He asked, "Who was the last person to get on the bus?" No one spoke. He then announced that he would fetch a policeman. While the conductress, driver and inspector were away looking for a policeman, a little man came up to the bus stop and asked, "Is this the bus to Stockport?" Hearing that it was, he got on. A few minutes later the three returned accompanied by a policeman. He asked, "What seems to be the trouble? Who was the last person to get on the bus?" The little man said, "I was." The policeman said, "All right, get off." All the people on the bus burst into laughter. The conductress, thinking they were laughing at her, burst into tears and said she refused

---

15. Cage, "Composition as Process, I. Changes", in: *Silence*, p. 32.

to make the trip to Stockport. The inspector then arranged for another conductress to take over. She, seeing the little man standing at the bus stop, said, "What are you doing there?" He said, "I am waiting to go to Stockport." She said, "Well, this is the bus to Stockport. Are you getting on or not?"[16]

1.5. CHANCE AS THE NEGATION OF INTENTION, AS THE NEGATION OF A SYSTEM

By way of conclusion regarding the importance of chance and non-intention in John Cage's approach, I shall mention a series of characteristics of chance that emphasize the non-intentional and asystematic. Those characteristics may appear to be definitions, or be viewed as consequences of other features. Although I shall try to avoid the term "systemlessness" in the following, one should bear in mind that it is always present; one exercise would therefore be to replace the word "chance" with "systemlessness".

1. Chance is a "non-system" for composing and for the creation of art, providing an infinite number of possibilities for the artist.

2. Chance is inherently open to all possibilities. This guarantees an open work of art, the work of art as a process. If chance operations provide a huge number of possibilities, the probability of repetition is reduced to nil, as is the likelihood of the formation of periodicity, i.e. of periods that will appear as repetitions or variations.

3. Chance is infinite. When using the "I Jing", for instance, one can keep throwing coins without ever expecting the end. What's more: it becomes extremely difficult to take a decision about the end of a work. The solution might be to let chance decide about the moment when the end occurs, which is what Cage did when he set the duration of his works or their performance.

---

16. Cage, "Indeterminacy", in: *Silence*, p. 271.

4. Chance is incomplete, unfinished. Given that the possibilities are endless, one can never say that a work of art resulting from chance operations is finished.

5. Chance cannot be commanded. Chance cannot be directed or pushed towards a certain goal. Chance has no sense of direction, there are no "road signs" leading the way.

6. Chance is unique.

7. Chance provides the best solution to a problem. This definition refers to the use of the *I Jing* as an oracle book. This is one of the first approaches to chance that Cage learned from Duchamp. Duchamp indeed used a coin to decide whether he would stay in Paris or fly to New York. He believed that chance would provide him with the best solution: one place indeed allowed him to do and experience things, meet people, etc., that were unlikely, or downright impossible in the other city.

8. "Chance is the abstract nature or quality shared by unexpected, random or unpredictable events.
Chance is probability.
Chance is an opportunity.
Chance is a risk.
Chance is a hazard.
Chance is a gamble."[17]

9. "Chance is the intersection of independent causal chains. Each is deterministic on its own, but the intersections create unthinkable complexity and inevitable unpredictability."[18] This can be clarified by looking at how a child relates to its

---

17. Hayles, "Chance Operations: Cagean Paradox and Contemporary Science", in: Perloff and Junkermann (eds), *John Cage, Composed in America*, p. 226.
These descriptions are quoted by Hayles from *The American Heritage Dictionary*. They refer to our experience of chance as something uncontrollable, something that lies beyond our expectations, anticipation and predictions.
18. Hayles, p. 227.

parents. The parents met by chance, which was admittedly infinitesimal and in fact depended on the same kind of chance that led to the meeting of their respective parents, etc. At a given moment ("by chance", if you will), those parents procreated a child, which was again the highly unpredictable (coincidental) result of their two sets of genes. One can therefore conclude that, according to the laws of probability, the likelihood of that particular child was infinitely small.

"Conjunctions between independent worldlines happen all the time. The point is not to deny connection, since conjunction is a kind of connection. Continuity in the strong sense of sequential events related through cause and effect, implies an ability to isolate the causal chains from external influences. Conjunction emphasizes connections that are unplanned and out of control. Numerous connections of encounters by chance seem to result in the ongoing process of the world as it is and the universe, as it is. The way Cage is using chance in art is an image of the world, a mirror of the universe. And that is a very traditional definition of art: a mirror of the world."

10. "Chance is characterized by non-compressibility" (see 6).[19] A good example of this is a series of randomly picked figures, which cannot be summarized, simplified or traced back to a shared starting point. This means that one cannot synthesize a series of chance operations, because there is no structuring principle, no hierarchy among the elements, no elements with shared qualities — no system. Incompressibility also encompasses a plenitude of information that excludes simplification. This might lead to an increase of information content as random content increases.

11. Chance is excluded at the very moment when it takes place, whereby "it" refers to a special event, which happens to take place at the same time. Yet, "it" could also refer to the decision one takes: chance disappears as soon as you decide to use one possibility.

---

19. ibid., p. 235.

2. MORTON FELDMAN
2.1. THE NATURE OF SYSTEMLESSNESS

Even though their works of the 1950s show certain similarities between the asystematic approach of Feldman and the way in which Cage handles chance, Feldman devised and used his own clearly defined set of techniques within the systemless, which are so fundamental that we can call them his personal aesthetics of systemlessness. A claim like the following is clearly related to chance: "Everything is a found object. Even something that I do invent is a found object. You're dealing with found objects. You're all amateur Duchamp, and you don't know it. And in realizing that, you must loose your vested interest in ideas".[20] It is sweeping in that it questions the development of compositional ideas. If the compositional ideas were indeed to be reduced to random ideas, Feldman destroys their claim of creativity and originality by stating that whatever you find already exists.

Feldman repeatedly condemned working with ideas, thus stressing that he worked from total freedom, without prepared concepts or predefined plans. Both his early and late texts contain remarks to this effect. The most fundamental refers to his introduction to John Cage in 1950, where he mentions a string quartet, later lost, of which he says that he doesn't remember the composition system and wherein he rejected the serial constraints of his entourage: "At the first meeting I brought John a string quartet. He looked at it a long time and then said, 'How did you make this?' I thought of my constant quarrels with Wolpe and also that, just a week before, after showing a composition of mine to Milton Babbitt and answering his questions as intelligently as I could, he said to me, 'Morton, I don't understand a word you're saying.' And so, in a very weak voice, I answered John, 'I don't know how I made it.' The response to this was startling. John jumped up and down and, with a kind of high monkey squeal, screeched, 'Isn't that marvelous. Isn't that wonderful. It's so beautiful, and he doesn't know how he made it.' Quite frankly, I sometimes wonder how my

---

20. Feldman, "Darmstadt Lecture 1984", in: *Essays*, p. 187.

music would have turned out if John had not given me those early permissions to have confidence in my instincts."[21] A few years before passing on, Feldman is still convinced that working from, or elaborating on ideas is something negative. During a lecture at Middelburg (Holland) in 1985,[22] he said that he really only went astray while composing if he didn't start from nothing, i.e. when he started thinking about ideas. He only feels safe in unchartered territory, because then he doesn't know he's getting lost. He states unequivocally that by searching for ideas, he would go astray in his own history: from a Cagean point of view, this is to be understood as his own limitation, the very thing Cage tried to escape from. In that same lecture, Feldman also said that he had no expectations whatsoever when he started composing a new piece. He certainly didn't expect anybody to understand it, and even stated that even he didn't understand some of his works, while those are exactly the ones other people call his "best" pieces. Consequently, he didn't even want to recall his own music: "How can I talk about my work? I'm intensely involved as I do it. And the minute I draw the double-bar line and I wake up the next morning, I hardly remember anything about it. It's over. A piece doesn't live when you finish it as a composer. When you draw the double-bar line, the piece is ended, finished. You know, I'm not a person who goes around and says 'my piece'".[23]

Nevertheless, Feldman assumes full responsibility for his music and tries to explain how he can compose without any system: "When I sit down and write a piece, I'm in thought. And as I'm moving, I'm focusing from one thought to another. And the whole idea of being in thought is to find the right kinds of notation at that moment that presents that thought".[24] He wants others to approach his works in the same way he writes them: by means of a simple statistic analysis, collecting facts, without trying to reach a synthesis or drawing general conclusions. That is why he never

---

21. Feldman, "Autobiography", in: *Essays*, p. 36.
22. Feldman, "Middelburg Vortrag", in: *Musik-Konzepte 48/49*, pp. 18–20.
23. Feldman, "Darmstadt Lecture 1984", in: *Essays*, p. 200.
24. ibid.

forgave that critic who claimed to have discovered new hierarchies in his *Piano* piece, because hierarchy is one of the worst things one can reflect upon from a theoretical point of view.[25] Even this last utterance indicates his desire to use systemlessness as a composition technique.

To Feldman, the asystematic refers to composing without any hierarchy whatsoever or preconceived concepts, let alone the elaboration of musical ideas. Furthermore, he is convinced that the composer should not have to justify himself for his works. So much for the negations, the statement that explains what not to do. Let us now move on and look at how systemlessness can be defined in an affirmative way. What he does define in a positive way is the concentration deployed while he is at work that allows him to devise a sequel to what he is working at at that precise moment. Such a sequel is not derived from what has already been done, nor is it a logical consequence. It merely refers to his moving from the preceding to the next.

On the whole, systemlessness seems to be fundamentally and permanently present in Feldman's aesthetics. That is not to say that he evolves in a straight line, like Cage does, towards an ever-higher degree of systemlessness. Feldman is not consistent: he sometimes creates scores where everything is written down in traditional form, then again "graph scores" (originally on "graph paper", hence the name). He sometimes works with indeterminate durations, only to decide to define everything next time around. Sometimes, the asystematic rules, at other times, his repetitions and variations of the motifs are elaborated in a structured way. Especially his discovery of Magrebinian tapestry in the 1970s caused him to work in a structured fashion, whereby repetition was the predominant element. Even though Feldman states that what characterized that period was that he never looked back on what he had already composed, the works he created during that period rely rather heavily on "techniques" based on the remembrance of and derivation from the preceding. The fact that

---

25. Feldman, "Middelburg Vortrag", in: *Musik-Konzepte 48/49*, p. 17.

Feldman decided not to return to what he had written before was his guarantee that he would never use literal repetitions but instead be creative, starting merely from what he had remembered from his preceding work, while continuing to write. Structure is therefore not to be confused with a pre-established plan; it is the act of composing with a strong awareness of construction. The structure emerges at the time of writing and remains free, meaning unpredictable. Feldman once again emphasizes that, rather than developing musical ideas, he moves from one moment to the next. That way, Feldman preserved a certain empathy for systemlessness in his more constructed works.

2.2. GRAPH NOTATION AND FREE DURATIONAL NOTATION IN THE 1950S AND '60S

The first "graph music", or "graph notation", was presumably written on 17 December 1950. The piece was called *Projection 1* for solo cello and was somehow indebted to John Cage, because Feldman mentioned that the piece had emerged by pure coincidence at Cage's house: "It was one of those discoveries whose importance only becomes clear at a later stage. I have no idea how I got that idea. At the time, I lived in the same building as John Cage, and he had invited me over for supper. John had cooked whole-grain rice in a rather unusual way. You need to wait until the water is boiling, after which you pour fresh water onto the rice. You take another pot to boil more water, you leave the rice to strain, etc., etc. The food took a long time coming. So I sat at Cage's desk, took a piece of paper and started drawing on it. I drew a free set of rectangles that revealed high, middle and low registers. I had no theory about it and did not know what the result would be, but if I hadn't waited for that whole-grain rice, I would never have had that wild idea."[26] Feldman provided this explanation with slight variations in various texts and during various lectures. What is important, however, is what he adds when he talks about *Projection 2* in his *Autobiography*: "My desire was

---

26. Claren, *Neither*, pp. 45-46.

not to 'compose', but to project sounds into time, free from a compositional rhetoric that had no place here. In order not to involve the performer (i.e., myself) in memory (relationships), and because the sounds no longer had an inherent symbolic shape, I allowed for indeterminacies in regard to pitch. In the 'Projections' only register (high, middle or low), time values and dynamics (soft throughout) were designated."[27] In that same text, he stresses that he never even considered his *Projections* to be a kind of improvisation. To him, it was "a totally abstract sonic adventure."

Ill. 3. Feldman, Projection 1, beginning.
A = arco   P = pizzicato   ◊ = harmonics

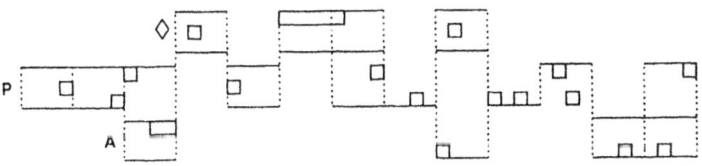

With respect to the asystematic, we need to take note of the following. The *Projections* (1950–51) were "found", not invented. They were not the result of a compositional system. From the composer's point of view, the act of creation was entirely free, "drawn" while not even thinking about composing music.

After notating it, Feldman decided to convert his "drawing" into music, i.e. to consider it a graphic score. Reading the drawing should therefore be considered an interpretation of the possibility to perform it musically. Why are the high, middle and low registers connected to the higher, intermediate and lower rectangles? This is not really necessary, unless one wishes to apply a convention whereby what is notated above should be related to higher-pitched sounds. But surely, Feldman could have specified this in some other way: at that stage, a general convention applies. And

---

27. Feldman, "Autobiography", in: *Essays*, p. 38.

why is this a cello piece? That was an arbitrary decision Feldman made after the fact of notation and without any connection to the notated. Maybe it was just because there was a cello player around. The same is true of his arco, pizzicato and harmonics, which he added later as an arbitrary decision.

In his free durational notation, to which the *Durations* (1961–62) and *Last Pieces for piano* (1959) series belong, Feldman attempts to work with independent, individual sounds. He tries to dissociate every sound from its predecessor and successor. To this end, he lets the performers decide about the duration of every sound: "In each piece the instruments begin simultaneously, and are then free to choose their own durations within a given general tempo. The sounds themselves are designated".[28] For the independence he wishes to achieve, Feldman uses the image of a kaleidoscope of sound when talking about *Durations 1*. "To achieve this I wrote each voice individually, choosing intervals that seemed to erase or cancel out each sound as soon as we hear the next."[29] Allow me to point out that Feldman deliberately uses "seemed to erase or cancel out", because he knows that this is impossible in the real world. Like *Projections*, the written image of *Durations* is alienated from the audible result. *Durations* are notated as a series of contemporary sounds, whose individual notes are written in perfect vertical lines. Yet, only the very first note needs to be played simultaneously, thus producing an intended harmony. From then on, thanks to the free duration of all sounds, polyphony emerges.

Those early compositions trigger important questions about the structure and perception of Feldman's music, and those same questions still apply to his later works. They also encourage us to be careful with an analytic approach, because the visual representation must not be considered the equivalent of the score of a traditional piece of music. The audible result does not correspond to what has been written down. In *Projections*, this can be inferred

---

28. ibid., p. 39.
29. ibid.

from the free pitch notation in various registers, in *Durations* even more dramatically from the polyphony that emerges during the performance, based on homorhythmic or chordal score notation. The performer's task plays an important part in the analysis. To perform Feldman in an "authentic" way, the performer needs to follow the composer's intentions: he or she will therefore not attempt to establish relationships between consecutive sounds, thus avoiding to impose unintended structures onto the listener. Any analysis of the written score is therefore extremely fragmentary, or downright misleading. An analysis of what is perceived, however, is a confinement to the analysis of one possible performance and can thus only be considered a reduction of free pitches or durations. On the other hand, while discussing Cage's "structure" element, I stated that structure is always present on the level of perception, and that the listener necessarily compares consecutive sounds with one another, thereby structuring them. The listener will indeed establish a relationship among unrelated sounds that he perceived consecutively. Does this mean that the asystematic is lost at the time of performance? Not necessarily, because the listener may well combine the sounds into a structure, without ever being able to discover a system in that structure, because there is no system. Within the theory of perception, several studies centered on "forgetting" asked the question: how long must a silence last after a sound for the listener to "forget" that sound before hearing the next, which is therefore not related to the preceding sound? Given Feldman's intentions, it would have been interesting to know the answer to that question. Yet, I believe it is irrelevant, because it is highly subjective to begin with, while, more importantly, "forgetfulness" can be excluded altogether from careful listening. Concentrating on the minimal presence of sound and countless silences in Feldman's music, the listener is almost certain to "remember" every single sound and to compare it with the next in line. I therefore do not believe in the theory of "forgetting", or the possibility to make music where it would be impossible to connect past sounds with subsequent ones. Nor do I agree with the idea that Feldman composed with the urge to contradict every possible expectation the listener might have, i.e. from a negative point of view. First of all, this cannot be checked: Feldman never even so much as hinted at doing it, which is why I believe he never did it. Secondly: if one used a large group, the sheer number of listeners might include all possibilities, so that there would always be someone who hears what he or she expects. If one considers only one octave, there are indeed only eleven possibilities after each tone, which is not a lot. On the other hand, Feldman also considered the octaves, the timbres in various registers in his compositions in order to reach the highest possible degree of differentiation and to increase unpredictability. Consequently, reductions, as exemplified a moment ago, are a highly dangerous procedure for the analysis of Feldman's works. They may indeed lead to senseless simplifications; it may distort or reduce the sound composed by Feldman to such an extent that everything seems to be based on extremely simple systems. And finally: I feel that the perception of Feldman's music is effectively dominated by the sound phenomena that are at work at each moment, whereby slow passages during long durations hamper or indeed prohibit the construction of a structure while listening. Feldman never used a negative approach in the sense of wondering how he could send the previous tone into oblivion; he used an affirmative approach by trying to make the next sound so rich that the preceding one would recede behind its "beauty", i.e. the unexpected, unpredictable, plus the wealth of the subsequently perceived sound, or quite simply the asystematic.

Oversimplifying reductions, and thus also wrong reasoning abound in several analyses edited by Thomas DeLio[30]. John Welsh, for one, analyses *Projection I*[31] and looks at the distribution of sounds within the various registers, the distribution of timbres (arco, pizzicato, harmonics) and the duration of the various tim-

---

30. DeLio, *The Music of Morton Feldman*.
31. From the very onset, Welsh makes a mistake while transcribing the piece in his own notation system and indicating a pizzicato sound in the high register as harmonic (DeLio, p. 22). He maintains that mistake in all subsequent steps of his analysis and in his conclusion. Welsh makes a second mistake with respect to the durations. Feldman's tempo indication read "MM = 72", meaning that each ictus or unit lasts 60/72nd of a minute, or 5/6ths of a second. Welsh, however, states that each ictus lasts one second (DeLio, p. 23).

bres. This leads Welsh to the following conclusion: "Feldman turns to timbre, density, register and silence for the structure of 'Projection 1'. The performer is free to choose any pitch and, as such, this parameter is irrelevant to the structure, which he has created. (...) As with all of his graphic scores, Feldman here creates a rich diversity of sound through statistical structuring. The compositional approach was, by its very nature, radical and led the composer to notate his works on graph paper instead of traditional musical staff paper." Those conclusions are at odds with my approach of this work described above. According to Welsh, Feldman indeed created a structure based on "statistical structuring" and even a "compositional approach", while the composer himself claims to have drawn something out of the blue. According to Welsh, pitch is irrelevant for the structure, while Feldman only interpreted pitch as registers after the facts. It strikes one as strange that Welsh didn't even consider Feldman's aesthetic and compositional approach. After such an example, one has little difficulty understanding why Feldman should ask musicologists to restrict themselves to "simple statistical analyses" of his works. When I make such a simple statistical analysis of the rectangles he drew, I come to the conclusion that Feldman, despite his freedom, used a fairly "normal" drawing technique: there are lots of squares on the (imagined) horizontal centerline; there is a climbing/falling tendency with increasing divergences from the beginning, so that the very high and low blocks reach "extremes". The same behavioral pattern also surfaces in the predominance of square blocks, which are obviously suggested by the "graph paper". There again, longer blocks are exceptions rather than the rule. Everything seems to correspond to a "normal" Gauss curve, which is something one expects when asked by someone else to draw random squares on graph paper. An analysis might take such a simple fact as a starting point, because it takes into account the way in which the composition (in its pre-compositional stage) came into being and respects its freedom and systemlessness. After that initial analysis, one might start looking at the elements that shape the timbres.

Ill. 4. Feldman, Last Pieces, n° 3.

In his analysis of *Last Piece n°3*, a composition with "free durational notation", DeLio tries to show to what extent that piece is constructed, thus running counter to Feldman's own aesthetic intention. Despite all that, DeLio proves in his introduction that he has indeed understood Feldman: "Rejecting the most basic tenets of conventional musical discourse, he moved toward a creative stance in which sounds appear to move freely in time and space without the interference of any compositional rhetoric or 'a priori' procedures. Each of his works represents a sensitive transcription of the creative moment. Indeed, one is often tempted to refer to his compositions not so much as pieces of music but rather as actions in the process of becoming musical works; as examples of one impulse toward the experience known as art."[32] Yet, right after that, he surrenders to "the various compositional procedures which are employed", only to find a rather "classic" solution: the first five notes constitute the nucleus of the entire composition, and that nucleus is then developed. That leads him to the conclusion that structure and hierarchy govern this music: "Each sonor-

---

32. DeLio, p. 39.

Systemlessness in Music

ity is played slowly and softly. At first, they appear isolated and unconnected. As the music proceeds, however, relationships proliferate and a clear hierarchy is established. Finally, meaningful horizontal connections are defined and the sonorities themselves are linked together over time. Thus, from apparently isolated, random events, a network of interconnections gradually emerges."[33] This becomes only possible, because DeLio reduces the intervals within each octave and because he considers complementary intervals to be identical. That is why he reduces the diversity of intervals to 1 to 6 possible semi-tones. Here is an example: the opening notes of the left and right hands in the first interval are D and F, which are four octaves and three semi-tones apart. DeLio reduces that to three semi-tones. DeLio's justification for doing so is "that is consistent with Feldman's usage. He never seems to systematically distinguish intervals from their inversions; rather, he usually treats them interchangeable; as different colorings of the same basic sonority".[34] Yet, it is precisely that coloring that matters to Feldman, because sounds, and even more so, concurrent sounds, become unique and independent by the very nature of their interval structure. As quoted above, "choosing intervals that seemed to erase or cancel out each sound as soon as we hear the next", to Feldman, means that the wealth of the next sound (including pitch, register, timbre, and of course, the interval with respect to the preceding sound) commands so much attention that the previous sound is "erased" rather than forgotten, i.e. the new sound is unique and more splendid than the preceding sound. Free duration may support this intention, but it doesn't guarantee it. The reductions introduced by DeLio allow him to conduct an analysis based on a mere three sets (usually incomplete, and therefore hardly ever identical sets). When Feldman claims to be concentrating on his acts of composing ("focusing from one thought to another", "being in thought") as quoted above, he must necessarily remember the opening notes of his piece, which explains why it is almost normal that similar nuclei should return throughout

---

33. ibid., p. 41.
34. ibid.

that piece. He most certainly did not build a structure from a nucleus of five chords, let alone from its simplest structural form, i.e. a recurring and slightly varied motif. DeLio thinks otherwise and thus believes he sees a "sonic language" that emerges as the piece evolves, which is precisely what he ends up stating[35]. DeLio must feel that something is strange, and therefore switches to the perception level. Even though Feldman never devised structures in a compositional sense, the listener will inevitably discover some. On the one hand, he quotes Feldman: "I'm very into acoustical reality. For me, there is no such thing as compositional reality", only to conclude: "thus, he creates structures in which order never seems imposed by the will of the composer, but rather, evolves within the perceiver's own awakening consciousness".[36] To me, that looks like an excuse given by a musicologist in order to preserve the consistency of his analysis. DeLio hides behind perception as a justification for his analysis, which, by the way, doesn't take perception as a starting point at all. After all, his analysis also relies on this simplification that excludes both the polyphony of the performance and its perception, concentrating instead on the intervals as they were written.

The fact that all sets DeLio claims to discover are incomplete, points to yet another aspect of Feldman's music, an aspect that also excludes structure, and which is emphasized by Herman Sabbe, who wrote an introduction for DeLio's book: "Feldman's music presents constantly differing degrees of difference and of similarity, in other words, a continual differentiation of difference — in still other words constantly altered degrees of similarity, exemplifying changing features or dimensions of the sound language. So, changes go many ways. They are unpredictable, constantly modifying or altogether defeating continuation hypotheses on the part of the listener — this unpredictability being enhanced by the well-known overall characteristics of the Feldman style: the generally slow temporal pace, low intensity level and ethereal timbral

---

35. DeLio, p. 56, repeated on p. 65.
36. ibid., p. 67.

weight. This is not to deny that there are connections among successive elements and figures in Feldman's music. They are, on the contrary, most definitely and continually. Only, they are not motivic — at least not in the original, etymological sense of 'motif' as a cause for motion, i.e. for immediate univocally directed action."[37] And then, Sabbe concludes: "So, the problem under consideration is how to describe, to rescribe, to verbally represent this music of no fixed musical-sense content, this music of continual change which is not reducible to any system — which, by the way, is why conventional methods of analysis, the very ones that are governed by principles of reduction, do not seem to be able to come to grips with this music."[38]

2.3. ABSTRACT EXPRESSIONISM

Feldman repeatedly hinted at the importance of Abstract Expressionism and of his friends, the painters of the New York School, for the development of his aesthetics and, more specifically, his systemlessness. Based on the example of painting, he wished to reach a world of sound that was more direct and physical, on the one hand, and more abstract, on the other.

This is first and foremost to do with simple parallels: like abstract painters, Feldman is extremely interested in the concept of a work of art as "surface": "My interest in 'surfaces' is the subject of my music. In that respect, my compositions are, in fact, no 'compositions'. One could compare them to a time canvas. I draw on that canvas with musical color. I have learned that the more one composes or builds, the more one obstructs unhampered time, the metaphor for becoming the controlling factor of music. Both terms, space and time, are used in music and plastic arts as well as in mathematics, literature, philosophy and science. (...) I prefer to think about my work as follows: between categories. Between time and space. Between painting and music. Between the construction

---

37. Sabbe, "The Feldman Paradoxes", in: DeLio, p. 9-10.
38. ibid., p. 10.

of music and its surfaces."[39] Feldman found another direct parallel in Jackson Pollock's action painting. Dripping as a technique freed the painter from traditional painting techniques. That action painting, a free way of painting, was exactly what Feldman wished to apply to sound, so as to project sounds as individual elements onto a score, without any relationship or score. "In thinking back to that time, I realize now how much the musical ideas I had in 1951 paralleled his mode of working. Pollock placed his canvas on the ground and painted as he walked around it. I put sheets of graph paper on the wall; each sheet framed the same time duration and was, in effect, a visual rhythmic structure. What resembled Pollock was my 'all over' approach to the time-canvas. Rather than the usual left-to-right passage across the page, the horizontal squares of the graph paper represented the tempo — with each box equal to a pre-established ictus; and the vertical squares were the instrumentation of the composition. As I came to know Pollock better, I began to see similar associations that I might explore in music."[40]

The *When is a painting finished?* discussion within the New York School had had such a strong impact on Feldman he kept referring to it until the end of his life: "Guston tells us he does not finish a painting but 'abandons it'. At what point does he abandon it? Is it perhaps at the moment when it might become a 'painting'? After all, it's not a 'painting' that the artist really wanted. There is a strange propaganda that because someone composes or paints, what he necessarily wants is music or a picture. Completion is not in tying things up, not in 'giving one's feelings', or 'telling a truth'. Completion is simply the perennial death of the artist. Isn't any masterpiece a death scene? Isn't that why we want to remember it, because the artist is looking back on something when it's too late, when it's all over, when we see it finally, as something we have lost?"[41] Philip Guston, for his part, stated that a "finished" painting

---

39. Feldman, "Zwischen den Kategorien" (orig. "Between Categories"), in: *Essays*, p. 84.
40. Feldman, "Crippled Symmetry", in: *Essays*, p. 136.
41. Feldman, "After Modernism", in: *Essays*, p. 107.

is really only a compromise and that the conditions for reaching such a compromise were not unimportant. Feldman wanted to be uncompromising, he wanted to create musical pieces rather than "compositions". In an altogether different context, the discussion centers on the same thoughts Cage had when he mused about how to end a piece that had been created by chance possibilities. The systemless excludes the notion of "finishing" a piece almost entirely.

Another point within the abstract is total freedom during the creation, a kind of freedom, which, in Feldman's case, can effectively be interpreted as systemlessness. "But what was really interesting about the Abstract Expressionists was the singularly *non*-polemical environment they created. One must understand this point; it is crucial to understand that Abstract Expressionism was not fighting the traditional historical position, not fighting authority, not fighting religion. This is what gives it that uniquely American tone; it did not inherit the polemical continuity of European art. Mondrian was a fanatic in the European tradition, Guston is merely a compulsive — quite another thing. Mondrian wanted to save the world. You have only to look at a Rothko to know that he wanted to save himself."[42]

The importance of the abstract for Feldman cannot be overstressed: he indeed broke up with several of his painter friends when they decided to return to the figurative. Even more important is his idea that the abstract needs to remain abstract and must never be shoved in a direction of picture-related interpretation: "The abstract is not involved with ideas. It is an inner process that continually appears and becomes familiar like another consciousness. The most difficult thing in an art experience is to keep intact this consciousness of the abstract. (…) There is a real fear of the Abstract, because one does not know its function. (…) The Abstract, or rather the Abstract Experience, is only one thing — a unity that leaves one perpetually speculating."[43] The ultimate

---

42. ibid., p. 102.
43. ibid., p. 103–104.

consequence of this obsession with the abstract leads Feldman to a complete paradox, which he explains from the point of view of a painter: "Franz Kline told me it was only rarely that color did not act as an intrusion into his painting. Guston, too, felt this. Most crucial to him was the immediacy of where the forms were placed; his color had to continually go through states of erasure to get to that visual rightness.

In music it is the instruments that produce the color. And for me, that instrumental color robs the *sound* of its immediacy. The instrument has become for me a stencil, the deceptive *likeness* of a sound. For the most part it exaggerates the sound, blurs it, makes it larger than life, gives it a meaning, an emphasis it does not have in my ear.

To think of a music without instruments, is, I agree, a little premature, a little too Balzacian. But I, for one, cannot dismiss this thought. In creating this indeterminate situation I began to feel that the sounds were not concerned with my ideas of symmetry and design, that they wanted to sing of other things. They wanted to live, and I was stifling them. It is not a question of a controlled or a de-controlled methodology. In both cases, it is a methodology. Something is being made. And to make something is to constrain it.

I have found no answer to this dilemma. My whole creative life is simply an attempt to adjust to it. There is very little concern, very little involvement with anything else. It seems to me that, in spite of our efforts to trammel it, music has already flown the coop … escaped. There is an old proverb: 'Man makes plans … God laughs'. 'The composer makes plans … Music laughs.'"[44] The consequence of this ultimate freedom, the systemless nature of the abstract is imperceptible sound, because an instrument's timbre only reduces the extremes, because composing a sound is a restrictive decision, and therefore a restriction of freedom and an impulse to think along systematic lines. Feldman's honest statement that he never found a solution to that dilemma is of the utmost importance. There is indeed no solution: not-sounding

---

44. ibid., p. 114.

music simply does not exist. The only way out would be potential sound, a sound that hasn't sounded yet and is therefore asystematic, as abstract as can be and utterly free, but inaudible. Feldman therefore turns to non-music: "Music is still based on just a few technical models. As soon as you leave them you are in an area of music not recognizable as such."[45]

And yet, by emphasizing the time element during the last decade of his life, he found a solution of sorts to this dilemma. In 1978, Feldman decided he was going to confine himself to writing music without any restrictions, without paying attention to, or feeling limited by the composition's duration, possible challenges for its performance with respect to the technical capability and endurance of the musicians, the expectations of the listeners, or a conventional concert situation. That explains why his pieces become extremely long: his Second String Quartet (1985), for one, lasts five hours. The notion of time changes in longer pieces. According to Feldman, one can listen for up to one hour in terms of form and construction, memorize and think; beyond that limit, it becomes impossible, because that's when the "scale" starts to dominate. Long duration therefore provides him with an escape route for structuring perception. "The question of *scale*, for me, precludes any concept of symmetry or asymmetry from affecting the eventual length of my music. As a composer I am involved with the contradiction in not having the sum of the parts equal the whole. The scale of what is actually being represented, whether it be of the whole or of the part, is a phenomenon unto itself. The reciprocity inherent in scale, in fact, has made me realize that musical forms and related processes are essentially only methods of arranging material and serve no other function than to aid one's memory."[46] Art Lange asks what the listener is able to hear when a perceptible continuity, structure or order is no longer there: "The meaning is in the sound and not in the explanation."[47]

---

45. Feldman, "The Anxiety of Art", in: *Essays*, p. 90.
46. Feldman, "Crippled Symmetry", in: *Essays*, p. 126.
47. Lange, *String Quartet II*, hat art 1441–1444.

3. WOLFGANG RIHM
3.1. SYSTEMLESSNESS AS A(N) (IM)POSSIBILITY

In my introduction, I already mentioned Rihm, who said to be looking for a work of art that could not be analyzed and had no intention to present his compositions with a method for analyzing them. Here's what Rihm says: "Oftentimes, an art form also tries to promote the form of its investigation. I really do not provide such a thing. One should always look for an entrance that was indicated by fascination. An un-fascinated person can do nothing; one needs to be attracted in one way or another to dealing with those things. There are no recipes. Depth analysis is necessary, structures need to be established, but not for the sake of receiving my approval afterwards: 'Ah, right, the scientist found it. I used thirteen sounds, then fourteen, and I divided the lot by twelve.' That's not how it works. (…)

I do not walk around, carrying a logo, which, in a sonic way, confirms what the presupposition already believes it can expect from me. It changes every time. And if one has a clear-cut expectation ('This time, he composed something tonal, while last time around he worked with noises…?'), I will shatter it. Through my way of handling the material — something I have become aware of (I do not exclude self-analysis) — I seem to show its meaning as something derived from life rather than from a separate stock. There is no material outside the artist. That has been my creed from the very beginning."[48] The fact that Rihm should be so flexible and swiftly change his way of writing and technique is therefore related to life. The "structure" of his life creeps into his music; he does not choose a "technique" for composing. Here, then, systemlessness should be taken to refer to an approach related to life, based on an organic stimulus.

Rihm does not say that un-analyzable works of art exist. Un-analyzability could be the result of the high degree of complexity of the composition systems used, where only the composer himself

---

48. Fricke, "Musik ist nie bei sich", in: *NZfM* (2002), 2, p. 53-54.

can provide the key for the analysis by reverse-composing the piece and analyzing it as he goes. Rihm is certainly not an adept of post-serialism or New Complexity. Un-analyzability could be caused by the absence of a composition system, i.e. by systemlessness. Yet Rihm never really confirms that he composes without a system, he rather doubts whether systemlessness is at all possible: "Maybe this could be something to cling to: for me, as a human being, it is impossible to create something artistic in an 'unorderly' way. Everything we do sorts itself out. All our deeds are derived from our own structures. The question is always: how is something arranged, how is it structured? That is precisely where artistic license is to be found: making ad hoc decisions about the WHAT and HOW. (...) Works of art are materialized free movements of our mind that is able to structure, and condemned to structure. Whenever we, the highly gifted, do away with a structure, we discover the next structure of a higher order."[49] This quote and the preceding one about un-analyzability are fairly recent (1999 and 2002 respectively). At the time, Rihm had reached a stage where he was even more fascinated by structure and form than before, which is exemplified by the compositions that ultimately led to (the various versions of) *Jagden und Formen* in the late 1990s. Before that time, in the 1980s, he had devoted his energy to finding ways of composing without any system. Andrew Clements wrote a comment for the booklet accompanying a 1991 CD release of the String Quartets nos. 3, 5 and 8 (1976, 1981-83, 1987-88 respectively), entitled *Without Maps*, which can be taken as a clear metaphor for working without a system. He also quoted Rihm: "Often as I write, I have the impression that the emerging piece is the articulated search for the piece. I believe that the freedom of artistic enterprise expresses itself above all in the setting down of individual events."[50] Even though the musical result is completely different from Feldman's endeavor, this idea of Rihm is akin to the aesthetics of his American colleague. Rihm considers the "journey" towards the composition, the process of

---

49. Rihm, "Notiz zu Ordnung und Freiheit", in: *Offene Enden*, p. 128.
50. Clements, "Without Maps", in: *String Quartets n°3, 5, 8*, p. 18.

creating it, essential. That journey takes place in almost complete freedom, without any predefined system or pre-concept, even without any rule or law. Rihm keeps emphasizing the intuitive dimension of his way of composing. That journey allows for the emergence of a work in its full structure-lessness and system-lessness. He clings to his musical freedom, thereby escaping from the sources of tradition that have shaped him, yet he never feels the need to forsake that tradition. Allusions and quotations are not at odds with the quest for free composition. In the 1970's, Rihm's paradigm was the exclusion of intellectualism and structuralism introduced by the generations before him. His music was searching for new expressiveness; his music flowed like a stream of emotions on a freely fluctuating structure. The main aspects of Rihm's music were subjectivity in the sense of intuition, spontaneity and impulsivity; a preference for the gestural, the grand and the sporadic. Yet, those aspects were never related to aesthetic simplification in the composer's mind. Rihm stresses that he wishes to be clear, communicable and comprehensible. But if one tries to express something as complex as emotion through music, the result will necessarily be a complex musical piece. On the other hand, the music will be much simpler whenever such complexity is unnecessary.

3.2. SYSTEMLESSNESS IN THE 1980S

In the 1980s, Rihm embarked on a thorough exploration of systemlessness, which leads to a predominance of his aesthetics. Two sources of influence appear to be crucial here: Luigi Nono and Antonin Artaud. If the aesthetics of Nono's last decade can be symbolically summarized as "fragments", a term I borrow from his string quartet *Fragmente — Stille, An Diotima*, it becomes easy to see why Rihm felt attracted to Nono. The fragmentary is not an aesthetic goal Nono strived for, but rather the result of a musical approach related to life. In the *Caminar*-pieces, Nono presented himself as a searching human being. Rihm has never worked in any other way than from life towards music. And while, before 1980, Rihm did so by questioning the tradition of music, alluding to 19th- and 20th-century composition principles, for example,

Nono helped him find a reduction to the essence of the language of music. That reduction is brief, laconic and concentrated: it is the fragmentation of the material to the essence of each individual sound, until reaching the border of silence. Rihm describes the act of composing as a coherent elaboration of movement in time with periods of expansion and contraction similar to the way we breathe. That leads him to elastic curves, moments of construction and dismantling, growth and decay, coming and going, but also fleetingness, implosion and breaking (falling into smithereens). That leaves no room for prepared structural plans, organic evolution or system-based logical processes, because Rihm believes that unexpected events bring art to life. At the same time, he likes elaborating musical ideas in all possible ways, until the exhaustion of sound or until the composer is entirely satisfied. That leads to a series of compositions based on the same ideas, sometimes even on the same musical material, like the *Chiffre* cycle (I-VIII, 1982–88, for varying ensembles), *Klangbeschreibung* (1982–87, three numbers). The titles already refer to the act of writing. Yet *Klangbeschreibung* is more than the writing itself, it is about "describing sounds", which is totally different from what one usually expects, i.e. the "composition of sounds". That is why a "cipher" ("chiffre") is not a figure but rather a sign, an icon Rihm uses in his attempt to shape each sound individually: "Every sound, a sculpture of itself".[51] In his comment for the CD release of *Klangbeschreibung*, Josef Häusler therefore writes: "The general nature of Rihm's musical idiom might usefully be compared to certain types of poetic speech consisting of single words and syllables placed side by side, seemingly at random, but which nonetheless somehow find their way to an organic inner unity. From an expressive point of view, the scope of these 'linguistic gestures' ranges from the most reserved isolation to berserk rage, and frequently contrasts two extremes directly with each other."[52] In other words: Rihm looks for systemlessness that abounds with expressiveness.

---

51. Häusler, *Morphonie, Klangbeschreibung*, p. 11.
52. ibid.

The second important influence on Rihm's works of the 1980s stems from Antonin Artaud's theatre concepts stated in *Le théâtre de la cruauté* and *Le théâtre et son double*. Rihm's most direct references to Artaud are to be found in the *Tutuguri* cycle (1980–83), *Die Eroberung von Mexico* (1987/91), which is described as "Musik/Theater nach Antonin Artaud", and in the various versions of *Séraphin* (1994/96), again derived from Artaud. Yet, there are also other compositions that exhibit the same frame of mind. *Tutuguri* is a "Poème dansé nach dem Gedicht 'Tutuguri' aus dem Hörspiel 'Pour en finir avec le jugement de Dieu' von Antonin Artaud". Rihm immediately felt attracted to it: "When I first read Artaud's text: stream of music, effusion of music. Like a magnet: a pile of music. Soon, not the poem, but the concept of Artaud's theatre will become the starting point."[53] Artaud indeed does not consider a play a creation of the author's brain, but a creation by nature itself, by real space. He is convinced that such a work of art will possess objective wealth and excess, while at the same time being severe and clear, as though it had been written by an author. That natural spontaneity simply cannot be tied to a system. To understand Rihm, it is important to return to his source and to quote Artaud in *Le Théâtre de Séraphin*:

> My aim is to attempt a terrible feminine. The cry of revolt trampled underfoot, of armed anxiety in war, and of revindication.
> It is like the lament of a gaping abyss. The wounded earth cries out, but voices rise up: they are the pit of the crying abyss.
> Neutral. Feminine. Masculine.
>
> To emit the cry I empty myself.
> Not of air but of the very power of sound.
> I set up my male body before me. And having hurled on it "The eye" of a horrible mensuration, I force it to reenter me part for part.
> (…)

---

53. Rihm, "Notizen zur Tutuguri-Musik", in: *Ausgesprochen, Band 2*, p. 326.

> The cry I have just emitted *is* a dream.
> But a dream that eats the dream.
> I am quite comfortable in the subterranean pit; I am breathing as I should—o marvel!—and it is I, the actor.
> The air around me is immense but closed, for the cave is walled in on all sides.
> I imitate a startled warrior who has fallen all alone into the depths of the earth and who cries out, seized with fear.
> Now the cry I have just emitted summons first a pit of silence, a self-contradictory silence, then the sound of a cataract, the noise of water – which is in order, for sound is linked to the theater.
> It is thus that, in all true theater, the comprehensible rhythm is brought forth.[54]

To Rihm, *Tutuguri* became ritual theatre with music as its ritual energy. He discovered that music was able to produce a theatre form that does not rely on a plot or the intricacies of dialogue, but rather on images and invocations. That is why Rihm can no longer imagine "cleaned" and polished dialogues in opera. Music theatre no longer needs to tell a story. Freed from that constraint, it can become total theatre. Rihm prefers to work with raw energy rather than polished dialogues and stories: images and screams, invocations and signs. A scream, or shout, is much more direct than a word, because a word describes, while a scream is the direct expression of an emotion. Rihm wanted to transport those typical features of Artaud's theatre to music: more nature than culture, more direct, even crude and cruel ("cruauté" also contains "cru"). The consequences for music are that the natural crudeness of sound cannot be subjected to a "culturally" imagined or devised structure. It needs to preserve its freedom, or to put it in another way: systems (as "cultural" elements) simply cannot be applied here. Via Artaud, Rihm comes to the conclusion that his aesthetic must be system-free. That systemlessness is based on the "Rohzustand", the raw/crude state of sound. Sound must be naked, unborn, not yet created, in a state where it is not yet music. This leads Rihm to a

---

54. Artaud, "The Seraphim Theater", (no pagination).

kind of impossible situation: the very act of composing indeed removes a sound from its "Rohzustand". That doesn't stop him from trying to compose as crudely as possible, from the first idea, from fragments, from rudimentary, unpolished sound material. Sound as scream, created on the spot, like magma. Music without structure, just a stream of sounds, crude and raw, not "composed". Rihm tries to describe this as working with a sound's "impulses", leaving a sound to its own rules, which is tantamount to allowing the rules underlying the nature of sound to dominate. He wishes to work with "sound-bodies" ("Klang-Körper"), whose convulsiveness trigger a melody, rhythm and timbre. "Creature sound is the hazy, unformed sound that we carry within us, the utterance of which always assists us in formulating that of which we are emotionally capable", says Rihm, and he adds: "The sound is an actor, its creation can be composed action and plot."[55] This leads Rihm to the following conclusion: "From a musical point of view, this means that one moves away from style, towards the sound itself, the pre-sound ("Vor-Ton"), the hope to end up in the never-heard ("im Niegehörten")."[56]

Ill. 5. Rihm, Chiffre VII, p. 1–2.

So much for the composer's description of his attempt to work freely and therefore without any system. Based on the *Chiffre* cycle, I shall try to establish how Rihm tries to compose as freely as possible. One of Rihm's often quoted statements describes his approach: it is about a direct and spontaneous composition act, writing down the ideas he has when he concentrates. Here again, one might point out an analogy with Feldman, yet whereas Feldman stated that he concentrated on sound and the idea of sound, Rihm wants to trigger emotions and be moved by "direct sound speech". What does correspond with Feldman, though, is that Rihm wants to work with a pattern-free musical language, a language that allows for free disposal of the individual musical facts that emerge spontaneously.

---

55. Rihm, "About Music Theatre", p. 23.
56. Rihm, "Notizen zur Tutuguri-Musik", in: *Ausgesprochen, Band 2*, p. 326.

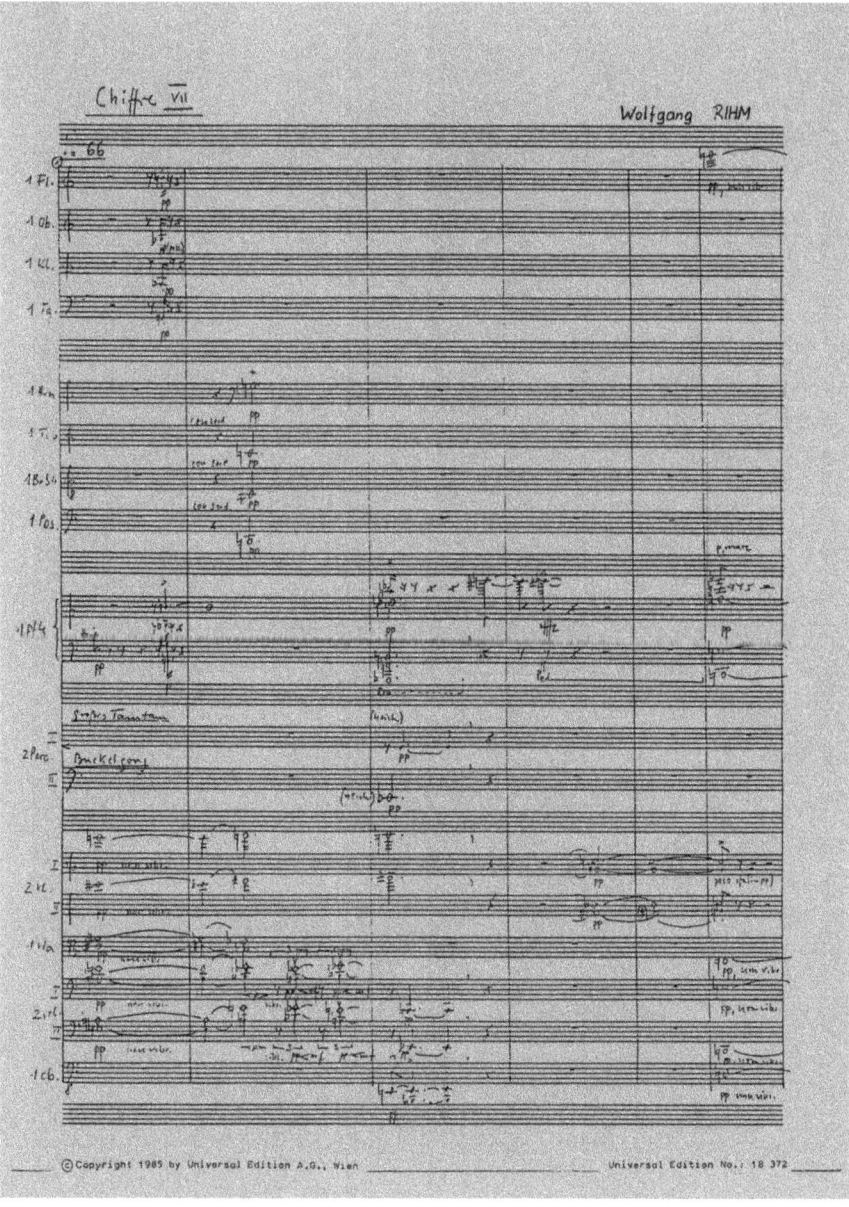

Ill. 5. Rihm, Chiffre VII, p. 1.

Ill. 5. Rihm, *Chiffre VII*, p. 2.

The following text was written at the occasion of *Chiffre VI*:

> What kinds of signs are these?
> What kind signature is this?
>
> First of all, one needs to rid oneself from the urge
> for cohesion to which one is subjected;
> radically break the ties of tradition,
> in which one resides,
> and move one step aside—
> stand radically next to it
> to see what is there.
>
> And at the time of writing:
> Do I know that? Don't I know that?
> What is it? What comes next
> if one doesn't plan beforehand
> or study the course—
> sit down in all liberty in front of a piece of paper
> not knowing what lies ahead;
> and still be responsible
> for precisely the tone
> that may follow next,
> for which one has to wait—
> for a long or short period of time;
> often so short that one cannot catch it,
> that one can no longer grab it while writing.[57]

Rihm believes that there will always be some kind of coherence in that spontaneous way of writing: by stating that, he can, of course, connect the systemless with his conclusion that everything man does is structured (see above), without creating a contradiction. To Rihm, systemlessness needs to be defined as the spontaneous creation of structures, no matter how loose or tight they are, similar to spontaneously writing down sounds. Rihm has repeated these

---

57. Rihm, "Chiffre VI", in: *Ausgesprochen, Band 2*, p. 342.

statements in endless variations. Allow me to quote one final statement taken from *Musical Freedom*, which was written 1983, when Rihm was in the middle of his *Chiffre* cycle: "If there is a tradition to which I feel I belong, then it is this: art as freedom to understand, born of freedom and committing to freedom. (…)

Art, the occupation with art and the making of art, is in itself already an invitation to limitless freedom. There can be no submission here, but nevertheless the law of the jungle applies brutally here, the survival of the strongest idea; any strategy is in vain, it may have certain results for a moment only, mostly of a market-relevant nature. A certain stoicism is by all means permitted here: whatever comes, comes. Any kind of kicking around works itself off. But this also means that, in this case, hope should not be placed in golden principles, in unchanging values of art, in the True, Beautiful, or even the Good. Uncertainty prevails, the only movement potential of the mind. It seems that the principles of the natural and vegetative must become manifest in the creative to the very extent that the surrounding nature is threatened and withdraws. This may also have been the case earlier, but art as counter-image is now expressed in a more plastic manner. This, I believe, is also the purpose of art: not to be a place of refuge in repressive times, but to serve as an energy tank. (…)

I believe in the unpredictability of art, in its completely individual unfolding, and ultimate inexplicability."

When one listens to the various parts of *Chiffre* and then looks at the scores, one first and foremost finds a kind of music that is directed at an immediate address from the "external": shocks and elements of surprise are usually related to dynamic, rhythmic (also tempo) and timbral elements. Timbres are often unusual because of the use of tremoli, harmonics, accents, etc. Rhythms are either irregular and unpredictable, or repeating patterns, or hammered repetitions. The dynamics with the aforesaid accents use extremes to their full extent, with the biggest possible oppositions. By contrast, the melodic and harmonic sequence remains on the same note cluster for some time, while chromatic neighbours are added for creating dissonance. A melodic gesture, for its part, can consist of the addition of chromatic neighbours to the droning chord,

Systemlessness in Music

which leads to a high degree of dissonance. Such a gesture may, however, also consist of revealing the elements present in a vertical chord. Rihm's occasional and sometimes (rather) long stops at one idea (signifying the impossibility to move on and the necessity to wait for the arrival of the next sound) indeed lead to the emergence of a spontaneous structure within the asystematic, thus corroborating his statement: no matter how hard one tries to be asystematic, one simple cannot produce something that has no order at all.

3.3. TOWARDS A NEW STRUCTURE

One of Rihm's major works from the 1990s is *Jagden und Formen*, which resulted from various earlier versions. Its precursors since 1995 were *Gejagte Form, Verborgene Form* and *Gedrängte Form*. The fact that Rihm should use the term "form" in the title hints at the importance of the problem of form, structure or construction, and by extension the composition system that generates those structures, for his compositional activities during the last decade. While, in the 1980s, the idea of the cycle was triggered by the elaboration of the same musical thought in various consecutive compositions, it is now based on overwriting the same composition time and again. Such overwriting cannot be reduced to re-writing, adaptation or replacement. Rihm considers it a palimpsest: a new version is added on top of the previous one. That way, a composition can be renewed by means of interpolations or added episodes, while other passages are left out. That principle is somehow akin to the technique of overpainting used by Arnulf Rainer, even though one has to be careful with such comparisons. It becomes nevertheless clear that Rihm is distancing himself from his spontaneous and asystematic 1980s. But he doesn't do that by returning to classical structures; he devises a new structural procedure, whereby the elaboration of the material plays an important part next to spontaneous discoveries of the material in the momentary idea. Rihm claims that an "original score" no longer exists, nor do an "original version" or a "unique work". He is far more concerned with the sheer quantity of possibilities, which he does not want to lose, just to preserve the unique moment of the idea. But he does cling to his spontaneity, by composing sections of his music in isolation, for example, without paying attention to the chronological order of those sections within the score: that only occurs at the end of the day.

A SERIES OF COMPARISONS BY WAY OF CONCLUSION

Throughout this paper, several comparisons have been made between Cage's, Feldman's and Rihm's approaches for applying systemlessness. By way of conclusion, I shall now elaborate on those comparisons.

1. Twentieth-century music in fact exhibits relatively few examples of systemlessness. Most composers prefer to work according to a system. Systemlessness is therefore not a widespread approach.

2. Among the composers studied above, composing without a system is tied to a specific period, after which the principle is abandoned (Rihm), or several periods interspersed with other approaches (Feldman). By combining systemlessness with the "system" of chance composition, Cage managed to find a solution for himself.

3. To Rihm, systemlessness is not isolated from the European tradition of expressiveness or expression music. Feldman views systemlessness as a function of abstract composition: as abstract as possible, and as distant as possible from any thought regarding expressiveness. Cage shares Feldman's point of view, which means that the United States and Europe are at odds with each other. Cage found a solution in the systemless nature of chance composition that allowed him to escape from personal expression in his music, which he considered a limitation. But with pieces like *0'00"*, he once again left a place for the subjectivity of the participating artists.

4. Within the systemless, the idea-related sits next to expression. Cage's point of view (other than the subjective element mentioned

above) is plain to see: his systemless music is neither thought up, nor invented. Ideas are of no importance whatsoever. The material is provided by chance. Feldman may claim that he cannot compose ideas, yet he also says that, while composing, he is "in thought", i.e. dealing with an idea. Yet he places one musical idea next to the other, he never establishes a relationship among them, he doesn't develop them. The same is true of Rihm: he waits for a flash, the musical idea, but he does not want to develop or elaborate it like a motif. Yet he allows it to develop itself. As long as it provides him with material from a free and spontaneous intuition, he continues to write around and with that idea.

5. Systemlessness opens up a wealth of possibilities: due to the absence of restrictive rules, freedom is almost boundless. Systemlessness even leads to non-compressibility; each moment is original and exclusive. Any reduction applied during an analysis would run counter to the music's spirit.

6. That does not mean that music resulting from such an approach is inherently complex. One conclusion applying to all three composers in fact shows the opposite: systemlessness is usually the onset for the creation of relatively simple music. In the light of his minimalist aesthetics, Feldman considers this an irrefutable fact. With respect to Cage, a piece like *4'33"*, in its (impracticable) most absolute performance, is the simplest musical piece ever written: one long silence. Yet, it is also complex in the light of its sociologic impact and its aesthetic consequences. Nevertheless, from a musical and technical point of view, it is a simple composition. Despite the stances Rihm takes with respect to complexity and simplicity, which are subject to the desirable clarity of expression, an approach of his music based on what one hears and finds while analyzing his scores seems to hint at a simple foundation. Furthermore, only by keeping it relatively simple can he succeed in his endeavor to create music with a direct and immediate impact on the listener.

7. The fact that Rihm should borrow the element of natural sound from Artaud inherently means that natural sound is less

complex than "culturally" developed or cultivated sound, whose possibilities have been explored by man. When this is projected onto "cultural" sound combinations, the difference between cultural arrangements and the simply natural becomes unbridgeable. Crude sound is simple, because of a severe lack of differentiation (otherwise, it would not be crude), yet its highly expressive content matters a lot more to Rihm. Whenever Cage turns to the "I Jing" principle as a way of thinking along the lines of probability, he digs into a distant eastern past, a stage when culture was still simple: the book *I Jing* was considered by everybody to contain wisdom, everybody believed in the oracular power of its statements. In that respect, I dare call it a simple cultural level that is still close to the natural. Cage's approach, too, is extremely simple: throwing coins with two possibilities each. Something similar can be said of Feldman: drawing squares and rectangles is something very simple.

8. Then, there is also this somewhat strange conclusion. By using systemlessness, all three composers leave the realm of music. Cage ended up creating works for performers who are no longer musicians, he stopped composing musical pieces. Feldman once said that the implementation of sound by means of an instrument seriously affected the degree of abstractness, by virtue of its timbre. He would have preferred working without instruments, and so with non-sounding music. Even though this is a theoretical conclusion, it nevertheless leads away from music. In his discussion of the "Vor-Ton", Rihm is still at a stage of uncomposed sound: it is a crude sound that has not yet been shaped in order to function within a composition. Again, this cannot be composed and leads him beyond music, to the imperceptible stage of the pre-compositional.

9. When systemlessness is composed, and becomes the trigger for a specific composition (be it on a traditional or graphic score) and a specific (unique) performance, it partially ceases to be systemless. Systemlessness can still be shown, yet the audible result will quickly lead musicologists and listeners to believe they dis-

covered structuring elements. From that point of view, systemlessness is far more virtual than real.

10. After all, systemlessness is primarily an idea, an intention or a philosophical consideration rather than a musical reality. That is something we find in all composers: there is a structure from which one cannot escape. The composer has no control over the listener and cannot keep him from structuring his perception. Rihm is most explicit about this; Cage stresses it in his self-analysis, based on structure, a method and a system. Especially in his criticism of Pollock, Feldman seems to indicate that freedom does not mean that structure has gone. One certainly senses it in his ongoing quest for the highest possible degree of abstraction, as a guarantee for not falling back on a structure based on a system.

11. All three composers start from a phenomenon (chance for Cage, the abstract for Feldman, the natural for Rihm) that is linked to matter, to the sound itself and that goes beyond that other "natural" element they create their composition for: man. I already mentioned that man structures by nature: if Rihm and Artaud talk about nature and the natural, that nature should not only be applied to the phenomenon of sound, or theatre, but also to man. Man's nature, apparently with his natural tendency to structure, undermines every attempt to be systemless; it tries to avoid systemlessness rather than look for it. The same is true of Cage: whenever Cage mentions chance as a fact in its own right, chance is immediately contradicted by man's natural tendency to put things in perspective. Same again for Feldman: if systemlessness is tied to the most extreme degree of abstraction, man's nature, with its tendency to make things concrete and palpable will contradict this inclination towards abstraction.

12. Finally: even though the goal of systemlessness is never reached in a satisfactory way, the degree of spontaneity and intuitive work can be said to be very high in Cage's, Feldman's and Rihm's endeavours. That is where their sensitivity for

systemlessness, and also its main implementation, lies. They may not be able to implement their intentions all the way, yet all three composers are fascinated by he highest possible degree of artistic freedom. Maybe that is how it should remain. After all, the fact that somebody should find a watertight system for composing in a systemless way that is both infinite and unlimited in the number of possibilities it offers, would either be a contradiction in its own right, or a mere coincidence.

BIBLIOGRAPHY

1. CAGE

John Cage: "Composition as Process", in: *Silence*, Middletown, Wesleyan University Press, 1973.

Katherine N. Hayles: "Chance Operations: Cagean Paradox and Contemporary Science", in: Marjorie Perloff and Charles Junkermann (eds), *John Cage, Composed in America*, Chicago & London, The University of Chicago Press, 1994.

Richard Kostelanetz: *John Cage*, New York, Praeger Publishers, 1970.

James Pritchett: *The Music of John Cage*, Cambridge University Press, 1993.

Stefan Schädler: "Transformationen des Zeitbegriffs in John Cages 'Music of Changes'", in: Heinz-Klaus Metzger and Rainer Riehn (eds): *John Cage II*, Musik-Konzepte, Sonderband, München, edition text + kritik, 1990.

2. FELDMAN

Sebastian Claren: *Neither, Die Musik Morton Feldmans*, Hofheim, Wolke, 2000.

Thomas DeLio: *The Music of Morton Feldman*, Westport (Connecticut), London, Greenwood Press, 1996.

Morton Feldman: *Essays*, Köln, Beginner Press, 1985.

Suzanne Josek: *The New York School*, Saarbrücken, PFAU, 1998.

Art Lange: CD booklet, *String Quartet II*, 2001, hat art 1441-1444.

Heinz-Klaus Metzger and Rainer Riehn (eds): *Morton Feldman*, Musik-Konzepte 48/49, München, edition text + kritik, 1986.

Walter Zimmermann: *Insel Musik, Desert Plants*, Köln, Beginner Press, 1981.

3. RIHM

Antonin Artaud: "The Seraphim Theater", in: CD booklet, *Die Eroberung von Mexico*, CPO 999 185-2.

Andrew Clements: CD booklet, *String Quartets n°3, 5, 8*, Montaigne 782001.

Stefan Fricke: "Musik ist nie bei sich", interview with Wolfgang Rihm, in: *Neue Zeitschrift für Musik* (2002), 2.

Josef Häusler: CD booklet, *Morphonie, Klangbeschreibung*, Hänssler Classic CD 93.010.

Wolfgang Rihm: *Ausgesprochen, Schriften und Gespräche*, Mainz, Schott, 1997.

Wolfgang Rihm: "About music theatre", in: *Janus* (2001), 7.

Wolfgang Rihm: *Offene Enden*, München, Hanser, 2002.

NATURE AND THE SUBLIME:
THE POLITICS OF ORDER AND DISORDER
IN TWENTIETH-CENTURY MUSIC

Max Paddison

"... there is a kind of collusion between capital and the avant-garde. The force of scepticism and even of destruction that capitalism has brought into play, and that Marx never ceased analysing and identifying, in some way encourages among artists a mistrust of established rules and a willingness to experiment with means of expression, with styles, with ever-new materials. There is something of the sublime in capitalist economy. It is not academic, it is not physiocratic, it admits of no nature. It is, in a sense, an economy regulated by an Idea — infinite wealth and power. It does not manage to present any example from reality to verify this Idea. In making science subordinate to itself through technologies, especially those of language, it only succeeds, on the contrary, in making reality increasingly ungraspable, subject to doubt, unsteady."[1]

INTRODUCTION

In the writings on aesthetics from the mid-eighteenth century there is a striking shift from a concept of nature associated with 'natural beauty', characterized by formal balance, clarity and order, to one associated with the natural sublime, characterized by the experience of formlessness, obscurity and disorder. This shift, which occurred as early as the 1750s, in particular in the famous treatise of Edmund Burke, *A Philosophical Enquiry into the Origin of our Ideas of the Sublime and the Beautiful* (1757), and which was dealt with systematically by Kant in his *Critique of Judgment* (1790), is the mark of the modern age well in advance of the aesthetic modernism of the twentieth century. Furthermore, while the idea of 'the sublime' has its origins in a certain overpowering

---

1. Lyotard, "The Sublime and the Avant-Garde", in: *The Inhuman: Reflections on Time*, p. 105.

and awe-inspiring experience of nature, it is, paradoxically, an experience that subsequently has come to occupy an equally societal domain. By this I mean that the overwhelming character of modern capitalist society comes to be experienced in terms of the 'natural sublime'. I mean this not only in the sense that in the early nineteenth century, for instance, people went out in their carriages to view battles from a safe distance, as if they were cataclysms of nature, but also in the sense that modern society, unlike the traditional community, is opaque and impossible to grasp in its totality because of its vastness and teeming complexity. In this paper I argue that there has been a further shift from the sublime as a set of experiences of nature (as overwhelming and awe-inspiring), via the experience of art (with autonomous avant-garde music, I suggest, as the epitome of the experience of the sublime), towards an experience of society characteristic of the modern world (that is, as the politics of the obscure, the overwhelming, and the extremely complex, within which the individual feels dwarfed and insignificant). This experience has been central to twentieth-century and contemporary music since such seminal works as Schoenberg's *Pierrot lunaire* and Stravinsky's *Le Sacre du printemps*. Although the sublime typifies the modern, and we have now seen its transference to the social and cultural domain, it is its relation to a contradictory concept of nature that is the focus of this paper. These two concepts, nature and the sublime, have powerful ideological implications, in the sense that they rest on a net of beliefs and assumptions of which we are only partly aware. The concept of nature, with all its imprecision and generality, has been — and remains — one of the strongest points of recourse for the justification of a wide range of aesthetic and political positions. In Adorno's words, such a concept of nature comes "closest to the concept of myth", and "is to be dissolved",[2] while the concept of the sublime, as Lyotard has put it, "is perhaps the only mode of aesthetic sensibility to characterize the modern".[3]

What follows has the character of an outline sketch for a larger project on music, nature and the sublime. It is necessarily incom-

---

2. Adorno, "The Idea of Natural-History", in: *Telos* 60.
3. Lyotard, "The Sublime and the Avant-Garde", p. 93.

plete at this stage, and restricts itself mainly to the clarification of concepts and the construction of categories, supported in some instances by reference to musical examples. I first put forward some key categories to distinguish different senses in which the concept of nature has been employed historically in relation to music. In the process of doing this I also consider some historically significant philosophical accounts of the concept of nature. Second, I suggest ways in which the shift from the natural sublime to what I am calling the 'constructed' sublime has been effected. My focus here is largely on twentieth-century and contemporary music, and my philosophical perspective draws in particular on Adorno and Lyotard, both of whom have made important connections between the avant-garde, the experience of modern capitalist society, and the sublime.

I. MUSIC AND THE IDEOLOGY OF NATURE: SOME HISTORICAL CATEGORIES

In the West, the view of what nature 'is' has shifted considerably at different historical periods. The English philosopher R.G. Collingwood, in his book *The Idea of Nature* (1945), has argued that there have been three fundamental shifts in European thought with regard to ideas of nature — the Greek, the Renaissance, and the Modern — and that these have been reflected in the forms of the science of nature based upon these views. I put them forward here in the context of this paper because I suggest that they still remain reflected in Western music and its theoretical discourses.

The first view, that of the ancient Greeks, Collingwood suggests, was characterized by the idea that the world of nature "is saturated or permeated by mind".[4] That is to say, matter is organic and animated by mind within it, it has its own intelligence, rationality, orderliness and regularity, and in this is part of a greater intelligence and orderliness. Thus 'nature', as *physis*, is the fusion of the physical world and a mind which is immanent to it.

---

4. Collingwood, *The Idea of Nature*, p. 5.

The second view, which is directly opposed to the Greek view, is misleadingly labeled the 'Renaissance' by Collingwood, and he in fact admits that he doesn't really mean the Renaissance in the historical sense, but rather the post-Renaissance period of the sixteenth and seventeenth centuries. This view, which is essentially Cartesian, is anti-organic, and sees nature as a machine, devoid of inherent life and intelligence of its own, at least in any independent sense. Nature is matter, 'stuff' acted upon by an intelligence external to it. This is the clockwork universe, set in motion by a superior intelligence, a divine creator, for a particular end, and therefore has a teleology. Although in motion, it is also static, in that, once set in movement, it does not change its course. It is an orderly and harmonious system, but the laws of nature are imposed and not immanent.

The third view, the Modern, sees nature by analogy with history. According to this view, argues Collingwood, nature is regarded, in contrast to the essentially static 'Renaissance' view, as a dynamic principle, a process of constant change, evolutionary and characterized by progress. It is Darwinian, but also, it has to be argued, Spencerian, in that it tends to view society and its artifacts in an evolutionary sense, by analogy with biology. According to Collingwood, the Modern view "is based on the analogy between the processes of the natural world as studied by natural scientists and the vicissitudes of human affairs as studied by historians".[5]

These three views are of interest here, not only because they represent three fundamental historical paradigms, each now historically displaced,[6] but because they also continue to occupy a kind of shadow existence and to exert a considerable influence on our thinking about nature, characterized as this is by contradictions. These three paradigms may be conveniently labeled the *organic intelligence*, the *orderly system*, and the *evolutionary principle*. While superseded, I suggest they live on — in music, at least. I have used Collingwood's model freely in conjunction with other familiar concepts like *imitation* and *representation* (and less familiar ones,

---

5. ibid., p. 9.
6. With the possible exception of the Modern view of nature, especially if it is understood in Hegelian terms rather than the social Darwinism implied by Collingwood.

like *embodiment* and *cognitive constraints*) to develop the following typological categories.

While there is clearly a certain amount of overlap, I suggest that each of these categories serves to identify distinctive sets of assumptions about the character of the relationship between music and nature. I argue that the influential notion that music *imitates* nature (whether organic, systematic or evolutionary) in some way or other is distinguishable from the idea that music *embodies* nature — the relationships are different, while at the same time there is a point where the two categories merge. Likewise the idea that music is the embodiment of natural laws, and is constrained by natural laws (for example, the laws of acoustics) is distinguishable from (although perhaps complemented by) the notion that the ways in which we are able to perceive music are dependent on the natural constraints of our physiology or psychology. And the view that music is not only constrained by and dependent upon natural laws but is also itself of natural origins and subject to some kind of evolutionary principle is clearly distinguishable from, and opposed to the view that music is none of these, but is rather a form of 'second' (as opposed to 'first') nature, and is subject to historico-cultural laws. I shall briefly consider each of these categories in turn.

I. MUSIC AS IMITATION OF NATURE

I suggest four main versions of the idea that music imitates, mimics or represents nature in some way. While each one of these can be understood on a relatively simple and elemental level, there is also a point reached in each when mimesis becomes complex, and the idea of nature as harmonious ideal moves in the direction of nature as threatening and overwhelming.

(1) music as mimesis of 'outer' nature (e.g. the imitation of natural phenomena)
(2) music as mimesis of 'inner' nature (e.g. the dynamics of feeling)
(3) music as mimesis of natural processes (e.g. organicism; imitation of nature 'in her manner of operation')

(4) music as representation of the idea of nature as the natural order of things, (e.g. the universe as orderly and harmonious system).

I shall not spend too much time here on the concept of mimesis — the idea that art is the imitation of nature (or anything else, for that matter) — although there remains much still to be said on art as imitation. It can, of course, be understood in a number of different ways. First, there is the very limited sense (for music at least) of art imitating natural phenomena. Perhaps the most spectacular example of this is Richard Strauss in his Alpine Symphony, with its waterfalls, sunrises and storms. Messiaen also persisted in pursuing the idea of representing nature in most of his music. The Introduction and the Coda of his *Chronochromie*, for example, contain indications in the score suggesting rocks, waterfalls and the wind, as well as the birdsong for which he is famous. However, once the idea of mimesis becomes the imitation of nature in its unpredictability, and in its cataclysmic aspects, or is transferred from nature to society also in its cataclysmic manifestations, then mimesis is in the territory of the sublime. Indeed, the sheer density and complexity of layer upon layer of birdsong in the sixth movement of *Chronochromie*, Epode, combined with the uniformity of tone-colour (a large number of solo strings playing in the upper register and minus the grounding of any bass line) and its duration (it's the longest movement in the work), is a somewhat extreme example of this. It is not 'cataclysmic' as such — in fact it has a strangely detached calmness about it — but it does create the sensation of hanging suspended over a chasm. It presents a simultaneity of extreme rapidity of movement with extreme stillness, forward motion at high speed with the total stasis of an eternal present. Such juxtapositions are disquieting, disorientating and vertiginous in a way that evokes the experience of the sublime. Second, there were the expanded possibilities offered by music as imitation in relation to the other arts, especially those involving words and gesture. This was originally at the relatively simple level of word painting or reminiscence techniques, but by the time of Berlioz in the first half of the nineteenth century the narrative being represented musically includes the nightmare of the opium dream or a Byronic journey through alpine landscapes. Third, there was the more complex notion of 'inner' nature being represented — something which leads to the aesthetics of expression in music. Intimately connected as this is to changing sensibilities and intensity of expressive needs, it rapidly arrives at the extremes of expressionism and neo-expressionism, and is again in that territory where formal conventions are overwhelmed, as an experience of terror and the sublime. And fourth, there was the idea of nature as the natural order of things, of the universe as orderly and harmonious system, which music in particular was able to represent, not only within any individual piece, but, indeed, as the whole system of music itself — e.g. tonality. In this case, it's not so much a matter of 'imitation' of nature, but more a matter of apparently 'being' nature itself. In this sense the idea of mimesis, in other respects distinguishable from it, merges with the idea of music as embodiment of nature. At the same time, the idea of a harmonious system also calls up deviations from the system existing simultaneously with the system itself. This may also lead to overwhelming structural complexity, a process to be seen in certain works of Stockhausen, and also of Brian Ferneyhough, where both system and deviations are created *ab initio*.

2. MUSIC AS EMBODIMENT OF NATURE

By 'embodiment' I wish to evoke the idea that music is itself in some way or other a direct manifestation of nature, rather than an imitation of it. I suggest the idea can be understood in the following senses:

(1) as natural laws (e.g. the systematic laws of acoustics)
(2) as natural material, 'raw stuff' of sound
(3) as natural, organic processes
(4) as cosmology.

The idea that music itself is a direct manifestation of 'natural laws', as, in particular, the laws of acoustics, is a pervasive one. It is, of course, questionable at best, in that Western music has rationalized the 'physical laws' of sound to such an extent, particularly to enable the tonal system to reach its full potential through modulations to distant keys, that it is now a highly artificial construct, dependent on a tuning system which finds it necessary to make considerable adjustments to the 'chord of nature', the harmonic series. The same can be said to apply to the idea that the material of music is in some way the natural 'raw stuff' of sound. In reality the material available to composers is the material passed on to them from other composers, and, as Adorno has argued persuasively, it is highly mediated and historically pre-formed. I shall return to this theme later in discussing the opposing positions of Schoenberg and Hindemith on these issues. The notion that musical compositions are like organisms in the way they unfold, and that they 'grow' from motivic-thematic 'seed-cells', is especially associated, of course, with a particular musical tradition — the Austro-German. The paradox of works from this tradition is that they are highly constructed artefacts designed to evoke the experience of nature. Finally, the idea of nature becomes the idea of world orders, of spheres interacting, and of cosmologies. If one were to follow up any one of these, and especially the last, with a musical case-study, one could do no better than to take Stockhausen's *Mantra* (1970), a piece which constructs its own worlds within worlds with level beyond level of allusion, detail and complexity.

Stockhausen's *Mantra* as World Order

This large-scale work lasts about an hour in performance, and is for two pianos, sine-wave generators, ring modulators, antique cymbals and woodblocks. It represents Stockhausen's return to a tonal world after his ground-breaking work of the 1950s and 1960s. But what Stockhausen does — post multiple serialism — is to recreate tonality from first principles, and in the process to create a cosmos where the large-scale principle (a 13-note melody with a tonal centre of A) permeates every detail. The melody in its original prime and inverted forms uses the chromatic scale, and is simultaneously a set, a 13-note row, presented using its inversion as accompaniment, albeit split into four re-permutated 'limbs'. In addition, and in parallel, Stockhausen creates twelve other 'artificial' scales, the intervals between the notes being stretched in each successive new scale, so that finally the scales cover the entire range of the piano. Each note in the melody also has a separate and distinctive characteristic—a mode of attack, a repetition, regular, aperiodic, a trill, a tremolo between two adjacent notes in the melody, and so on. The large-scale structure has thirteen large sections, each focused on a new pair of tonics (prime and its inversion) dictated by the succession of pitches in the melody, and each dominated texturally by the distinctive characteristic of its particular prime-form tonic. The two tonics in each section are constantly present, but not heard as such directly, as they are ghosted by sine-wave generated tones which are only audible directly at a few key moments, while for the rest of the time they are only 'heard' as a result of their effect on the totality through being fed into two ring modulators (one for each piano), together with the sounds played by the pianos. The resulting sound is unpredictable in its detail, even to Stockhausen, and has something in common with the sound of Cage's prepared piano. This also introduces an element of change and the unforeseen into what is in all other respects a highly organized structure—chance as a necessary and inevitable aspect of any world. What Stockhausen has created is a complete cosmos, with its own world order, but one which also relates to our world on many levels, not least in the way that each section of the work evokes a complete sound-world powerfully calling up different parts of our world—stride piano playing, Balinese gamelan, Japanese gagaku, and so on. It is not 'nature', of course, but it does conjure up through the sheer density of its highly-constructed complexity a vision of nature which operates on many different levels simultaneously, all being aspects of the same single principle. Indeed, it calls to mind John Cage's dictum in his 1961 article "On Robert Rauschenberg, Artist, and his Work": "To change the subject: 'Art is the imitation of nature in her manner of operation'. Or a net".[7] What Stockhausen has done, I suggest, is not only to imitate nature in its tiniest detail, but also to embody it in the most concrete terms possible. For Stockhausen, it is not that the piece *is* nature, or that it is a manifestation of natural laws, but that it constructs, sustains and

---

7. Cage, *Silence*, p. 100.

validates a world simultaneously incorporating elements of chance and deviation.

Hindemith, Schoenberg and the nature of musical material

The idea of music not only as the systematic manifestation of natural laws, but also as cosmology has been used to validate whole systems of music, in terms of scales, modes, intervals, and so on. Zarlino justified the system in this way, and likewise Rameau in his *Traité de l'harmonie réduite à ses principes naturels* (1722). After the breakdown of tonality (that is, the system essentially as defined and justified by Rameau), a debate broke out in the early twentieth century concerning music and nature. On the one side were those who tried to justify their own attempts to replace tonality as having natural foundations, and on the other those who argued that such claims on nature were spurious and unnecessary. These two extreme positions are well represented by Hindemith and Schoenberg. Hindemith in his theoretical text *The Craft of Musical Composition* (*Unterweisung im Tonsatz*) (2 vols., 1937) put forward the principles of his mature musical language in terms that emphasized "basic principles of composition, derived from the natural characteristics of tones, and consequently valid for all periods ... proceeding from the firm foundation of the laws of nature".[8] There is a clear emphasis on 'natural laws', and on the idea that there is a universal response, across history and different cultures, to the fixed meanings of the individual intervals. He claims that the major triad, for instance, "is ... one of the most impressive phenomena of Nature, simple and elemental as rain, snow, and wind". Indeed, Hindemith takes his analogy further: "In the world of tones, the triad corresponds to the force of gravity. It serves as our constant guiding point, our unit of measure, and our goal, in even those sections of compositions which avoid it."[9] He attributes a fixed value to each interval, according to the degree of tension he considers it to contain, and rationally derived, he claims, from the overtone series (the 'chord of nature'). His

---

8. Hindemith, *The Craft of Musical Composition*, p. 9.
9. ibid., p. 22.

position, founded on a vision of music as the embodiment of static, immutable and universal truths rooted in the eternal laws of nature, can be summarized most concisely in his own words: "we have seen that tonal relations are founded in Nature, in the characteristics of sounding materials and of the ear, as in the pure relations of abstract numerical groups. We cannot escape the relationship of tones ... Tonality is a natural force, like gravity".[10]

Hindemith was, of course, indirectly polemicising against the atonality and, in particular, the twelve-tone technique of Schoenberg, Berg and Webern, which he regarded as 'unnatural'. It is illuminating, therefore, to turn to Schoenberg to get the opposite position, as presented in his first, and perhaps most important theoretical work, his *Theory of Harmony* (*Harmonielehre*) (1911). Schoenberg insists that the so-called 'natural' laws of tonality are actually historical and conventional in character. In fact he even refers to the scale systems of other cultures to make his point that we can all appeal to nature to justify a system that is really just a historical convenience:

> The way of history, as we can see it in that which has actually been selected by practice from the practicable dissonances, hardly leads here to a correct judgment of the real relations. That assertion is proved by the incomplete or unusual scales of many other peoples, who have, nevertheless, as much right as we to explain them by appeal to nature. Perhaps their tones are often more natural than ours (that is, more exact, more correct, better); for the tempered system, which is only an expedient for overcoming the difficulties of the material, has indeed only a limited similarity to nature. That is perhaps an advantage, but hardly a mark of superiority.[11]

For Schoenberg, what we take to be natural laws are actually the result of "the struggle of the craftsman to shape the material correctly".[12] He also suggests that it is not natural forces to which the artist responds, but historical forces. And furthermore, he also

---

10. ibid., p. 152.
11. Schoenberg, *Theory of Harmony*, pp. 314–15.
12. ibid., p. 29.

argues that the way in which we hear music is also historically conditioned: "our present-day ear has been educated not only by the conditions nature imposed upon it, but also by those produced by the system, which has become a second nature".[13] I shall return to the idea of 'second nature' later in relation to Lukács and Adorno. For the moment, however, what is clear from Hindemith's theory is that it argues not only that musical material, as 'stuff', is subject to natural laws, but also that there are physiological, psychological and, indeed, social and communal restraints on the ways in which we are able to make sense of sounds, and that these constraints are also in some way natural. This calls for further examination, and cannot, of course, remain unchallenged.

3. MUSIC AND NATURAL CONSTRAINTS

The idea that music must conform to the constraints of our physiological, psychological and, ultimately, social make-up can be traced, at least in part, to the Kantian position that we can only experience and know the world in the way that we do because of the limits of our cognitive and perceptual faculties. At the same time, however, attempts to draw the outer limits of such constraints can easily appear arbitrary and historically contingent. I offer the following categories of 'constraint', including the notion of musical 'archetypes' which are deemed to correspond to the constraints of our perceptual apparatus.

(1) physiological constraints (e.g. the physiology of the ear)
(2) psychological constraints
(3) cultural constraints
(4) archetypes

L.B. Meyer, archetypes and cognitive constraints

The American aesthetician and musicologist, Leonard B. Meyer, explores the idea of cultural conventions in relation to 'natural'

---

13. ibid., p. 48.

cognitive constraints. He is interested in the notion of invariant archetypes, as he calls them, underlying the surface appearance of innovation. For Meyer the archetype in this sense is a fundamental pattern, a schema. He argues that archetypes are part of the 'competent listener's' psychological response patterns, and that they enable cultural continuity to take place in what he implies is an almost biological process. In fact, he also talks of archetypes as "the cognitive-mnemonic schemas that Richard Dawkins called 'memes'", as "biological trait transmission".[14] For Meyer, the role of nature is to be seen in the form of 'human cognitive constraints'. It is through our natural cognitive constraints that "the necessary conditions for replication" become established, "thereby making it possible for a particular pattern to become a convention".[15] The other side of his argument concerns the sufficient conditions: "that is, the cultural conditions that induce the compositional community to replicate particular patterns so that they actually become conventions".[16] It has to be said that there are problems with such a concept of musical nature. In my view, Meyer (like Hindemith) risks absolutizing cognitive capacities as 'nature' without sufficiently acknowledging the extent to which these 'cognitive constraints' are mediated by cultural/historical constraints. Likewise when we examine his concept of 'cultural constraints' we cannot help but notice the extent to which the cultural has been naturalized, so that cultural constraints come to bear a striking resemblance to cognitive constraints. In the absence of a concept of 'second nature' — a point interestingly made by Schoenberg in the extract cited earlier — Meyer reifies the idea of cognitive constraints, as he does his concept of archetypes.

Lukács, nature and second nature

The concept of 'second nature' is one also employed by the Hungarian literary theorist and culture critic, Georg Lukács. He argued in his *Theory of the Novel* (1916) that what we take as nature

---

14. Meyer, *The Spheres of Music: A Gathering of Essays*, p. 195. See also my review of Meyer in *Musicae Scientiae*, pp. 279-86.
15. ibid., p. 229.
16. ibid.

is, in fact, a 'second nature' of our own making. He sees it as the projection of our own unrecognized needs upon what we take as nature, but which is really only our own estrangement, or alienation, from the world we have constructed for ourselves. In a later work, in 1922, he asserted simply that "nature is a societal category". He went on to amplify this by saying that "whatever is held to be natural at any given stage of social development, however this nature is related to man and whatever form his involvement with it takes, i.e. nature's form, its content, its range and its objectivity are all socially conditioned".[17] The concepts of reification and second nature will inevitably lead us to a consideration of the position of the Frankfurt School, and to the important concept of mediation seen in the relationship of history/culture to myth. But first, a brief detour to consider the evolutionist position on the origins, development and teleology of music.

4. MUSIC, NATURAL ORIGINS AND TELEOLOGY

There are several different but related strands here, and I put forward the following four categories. The key factors are a concern with the beginnings of music in some natural biological or social function, and then a conviction that music 'evolves' in some way — becoming better adapted to its context, more complex, and possibly with some kind of historical teleology.

(1) natural origins of music (e.g. animal cries)
(2) natural evolution of music
(3) natural functions of music
(4) natural history of music

Darwin, Spencer, natural origins and evolution

Both Darwin and Spencer had some interest in the origins of music. Darwin originally suggested in *The Origin of Species* that music had its origins in the amatory calls and displays of animals.

---

17. Lukács, *History and Class Consciousness*, p. 234.

Later, in *The Expression of the Emotions in Man and Animals* (1872), he proposed that speech had its origins in the utterance of expressive musical sounds, and that "when the voice is used under any strong emotion, it tends to assume, through the principle of association, a musical character".[18] In fact, Darwin was by this time influenced in his views on music by Spencer's essay "The Origin and Function of Music" (1857)[19], while Spencer was sceptical of Darwin's hypothesis on the sexual origins of music, preferring a more general theory of expression. Spencer's Social Darwinist approach came to have a considerable influence on music histories in the late nineteenth and early twentieth centuries, particularly in Britain (as a glance at editions of the *Grove Dictionary of Music and Musicians* of that period will quickly demonstrate), and also on views of music's social function. The concern with music's origins in terms of some kind of natural, biological function persists, however, even though it does not tell us anything about what music has now become. Likewise, evolutionary theories of music history fail to account for the fact that in many ways much earlier music is more complex than much later music. Such theories also usually deal with 'music' at a level of generality and abstraction which is disrupted by the disjunct histories of different musics and, importantly, of particular works. As Adorno has argued on the question of origins: "The effort to subsume the historical genesis of art ontologically under an ultimate motif would necessarily flounder in such disparate material that the theory would emerge empty handed except for the obviously relevant insight that the arts will not fit into any gapless concept of art."[20]

Natural History and the Dialectic of Enlightenment: Benjamin, Adorno, Horkheimer

The remaining category, that of 'natural history', is associated particularly with Walter Benjamin and also Adorno. It differs from

---

18. Darwin, *The Expression of the Emotions in Man and Animals*, p. 92.
19. Spencer, "The Origin and Function of Music", in: *Literary Style and Music*, pp. 45–106., see especially pp. 76–88.
20. Adorno, *Aesthetic Theory*, p. 2.

the others so far considered, in that it is a *critical* rather than a descriptive or prescriptive concept, in that it compels us to re-examine our assumptions about the idea of nature. It applies to objects that have become 'naturalized' — cultural objects 'fallen into a state of nature' but which can also be deciphered and their cultural significance read. Indeed, there is a sense in which Benjamin's concept of 'natural history' sets out to demythologize the myth of nature and to reveal its cultural/historical significance. Adorno and Horkheimer also set out to achieve this in their book *Dialectic of Enlightenment* (1944). In the "Odysseus or Myth and Enlightenment" chapter they write:

> The opposition of enlightenment to myth is expressed in the opposition of the surviving individual [self] to multifarious fate. The eventful voyage from Troy to Ithaca is the way taken through the myths by the self — ever physically weak as against the power of nature, and attaining self-realization only in self-consciousness.[21]

I have represented the position of Benjamin, Adorno and Horkheimer on nature and history, myth and enlightenment, in Diagram I.[22]

A few words are needed to explain the diagram and the polarities represented in it. The four key terms *Myth↔Enlightenment* and *Nature↔History(Culture)* are to be understood as relative to each other, in that they are mediated through each other. That is to say, whatever 'nature' is, it is certainly mediated historically, to the extent that each historical period sees the nature it needs or wants, a nature which acts as a mirror to the gaze of history. To that extent it can be said that 'nature' is not a given, a static absolute, beyond history, but is itself historical and subject to change. On the other hand, history (or perhaps a better term in the English-

---

21. Adorno, *Dialectic of Enlightenment* (1944), trans. John Cumming (London: Verso, 1979), p. 46.
22. This diagram is a slightly adapted version of that which originally appeared in my *Adorno, Modernism and Mass Culture*, rev. ed. 2004, p. 26.

Diagram I.
                    Culture as a historical project

       Context: 18th-Century European Enlightenment and its consequences

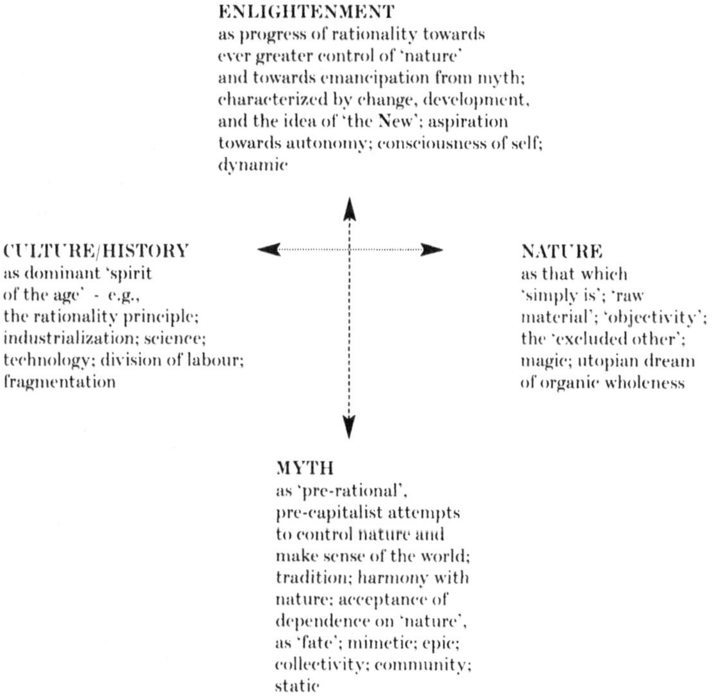

ENLIGHTENMENT
as progress of rationality towards ever greater control of 'nature' and towards emancipation from myth; characterized by change, development, and the idea of 'the New'; aspiration towards autonomy; consciousness of self; dynamic

CULTURE/HISTORY ⟷ **NATURE**

CULTURE/HISTORY
as dominant 'spirit of the age' - e.g., the rationality principle; industrialization; science; technology; division of labour; fragmentation

NATURE
as that which 'simply is'; 'raw material'; 'objectivity'; the 'excluded other'; magic; utopian dream of organic wholeness

MYTH
as 'pre-rational', pre-capitalist attempts to control nature and make sense of the world; tradition; harmony with nature; acceptance of dependence on 'nature', as 'fate'; mimetic; epic; collectivity; community; static

speaking world is *culture*, in the anthropological sense of the term) comes to be perceived not as constant dynamic change and flux, but instead as fixed and static, as a given. In becoming reified it becomes 'naturalized'. In this way one can understand that the opposites *Nature↔History(Culture)* are mediated through each other, each term having meaning only in relation to the other. Another way of looking at it is to say that our conception of nature is inevitably culturally constructed, while our way of relating to our culture is to naturalize it.

The *Myth↔Enlightenment* axis invites a similar interpretation. The eighteenth-century Enlightenment was characterized by belief in the progress of rationality towards ever greater control of nature and emancipation from myth. It is developmental and involved in a constant process of change in its search for the New. Myth is pre-rational and characterized by repetition and stasis. However, myth also seeks to control nature, but through magic and mimesis. Adorno and Horkheimer argue in *Dialectic of Enlightenment* that rationality and the process of rationalization that characterize the Enlightenment have their origins in the mythic attempt to control nature—a development which also led to emancipation from myth. They also go on to argue that rationality has now turned back on itself through its loss of critical reflexion and has regressed to myth. The nightmare underside of Enlightenment is the Holocaust.

INTERIM CONCLUSIONS

I suggest that two apparently opposing positions on nature stand out. The first position sees nature as objective orderly system, its categories mirrored in the individual subject and its creations. The second regards nature as chaotic force, threatening to overwhelm the identity of the individual subject as the experience of disorder, terror, unintelligibility and formlessness, in which respect it opens on to the experience of the sublime. The two positions are related. As Adorno suggests: "The enlightenment concept of nature contributed to the invasion of the sublime into art."[23] He also suggests that it was the overwhelming social upheaval of the French Revolution which acted as catalyst for this invasion of art by the sublime. What was originally a category of the experience of nature now becomes also a category of the experience of society.

II. THE POLITICS OF THE SUBLIME

I shall develop the context constructed in Part I around the concept of nature, in order to discuss the concept of the sublime. I will start by revisiting the observation by Lyotard that: "The sublime is perhaps the only mode of artistic sensibility to characterize the modern"[24]—a point he has derived from Adorno. Here I

---

23. Adorno, *Aesthetic Theory*, p. 196.
24. Lyotard, "The Sublime and the Avant-Garde", p. 93.

argue that the experience of the sublime which so characterizes our experience of art—and, indeed, for better or worse, our experience of the world—is the extreme extension of notions of order and disorder put forward in Part II in relation to the concept of nature, and calls for corresponding reflexion on the ideological implications it contains. Order, taken to its extreme through the process of increasing rationalization of all aspects of a structure, leads to forms of great density and complexity—what Kant called 'the mathematical sublime'—forms which must also attempt to incorporate disorder, chaos, chance and indeterminacy. Such densely ordered structures also provoke an immediate experience of unintelligibility (that is, they resist our capacity to grasp and make sense of the whole, which is overwhelming), akin to the experience of the sublime in both its 'natural' and its 'societal' aspects. A further point of orientation is Lyotard's assertion in discussing Kant's Analytic of the Sublime: "The sublime denies the imagination the power of forms, and denies nature the power to immediately affect thinking with forms."[25] This has political as well as aesthetic aspects.

I. THE CONCEPT OF THE SUBLIME: AN HISTORICAL OVERVIEW

The idea of the Sublime in art goes back to a 1st or 2nd century Greek treatise on rhetoric, attributed to Longinus, *On the Sublime*. This discusses the 'lofty style' of writing which 'ravishes and transports', and which is like a force of nature in its effect. The idea was taken up in the seventeenth century, after a rediscovery of Longinus, and came into its own in the eighteenth century, particularly in the writings of the philosophers Joseph Addison and, later, Edmund Burke. In his treatise *A Philosophical Enquiry into the Origin of our Ideas of the Sublime and Beautiful*, Burke defines the sublime in the following terms:

> Whatever is fitted in any sort to excite the ideas of pain, and danger, that is to say, whatever is in any sort terrible, or is conversant about terrible

---

25. Lyotard, *Lessons on the Analytic of the Sublime*, p. 54.

> objects, or operates in a manner analogous to terror, is a source of the *sublime*; that is, it is productive of the strongest emotion which the mind is capable of feeling.[26]

And at the opening of Part Two of his treatise Burke writes:

> The passion caused by the great and sublime in *nature*, when those causes operate most powerfully, is Astonishment; and astonishment is that state of the soul, in which all its motions are suspended, with some degree of horror. In this case the mind is so entirely filled with its object, that it cannot entertain any other, nor by consequence reason on that object which employs it. Hence arises the great power of the sublime, that far from being produced by them, it anticipates our reasonings, and hurries us on by an irresistible force. Astonishment, as I have said, is the effect of the sublime in its highest degree; the inferior effects are admiration, reverence and respect.[27]

The sublime gave rise to the fashion for wild landscapes, ruins, Gothic horror stories and the stupendous effects of nature, like thunderstorms and volcanoes. Kant, who devoted a whole section of his *Critique of Judgment* to the concept, treats it in the following terms:

> consider bold, overhanging and, as it were, threatening rocks, thunderclouds piling up in the sky and moving about accompanied by lightning and thunderclaps, volcanoes with all their destructive power, hurricanes with all the devastation they leave behind, the boundless ocean heaved up, the high waterfall of a mighty river, and so on. Compared to the might of any of these, our ability to resist becomes an insignificant trifle. Yet the sight of them becomes all the more attractive the more fearful it is, provided we are in a safe place. And we like to call these objects sublime because they raise the soul's fortitude above its usual middle range and allow us to discover in ourselves an ability to resist which is of a quite different kind, and which gives us the courage [to believe] that we could be a match for nature's seeming omnipotence.[28]

---

26. Burke, *A Philosophical Enquiry into the Origin of our Ideas of the Sublime and Beautiful*, p. 37.
27. ibid., p. 53.
28. Kant, *Critique of Judgment*, p. 120.

Nature and the Sublime

The sublime, according to Kant, refers to awe and terror in the face of the vastness of nature, where we become aware simultaneously of our own insignificance. Nevertheless, it is also an agreeable terror, so long as we know we are safe. It is this experience (which Kant distinguishes from that of Natural Beauty, because Beauty has form and purpose, whereas the Sublime cannot be grasped in these terms) which is also taken into the experience of art. The discussion as to what exactly can be understood under the concept of the sublime in music of this period—whether, for instance, Beethoven's *Eroica* or his Ninth Symphony would have been heard as examples of this by his contemporaries—are ultimately beside the point for my purposes at the moment. What also needs to be emphasized is that Kant presents an important, but at the same time derivative and even circumscribed account of the sublime. (I have in mind here the fact that the concept had been extensively discussed in the British writers on the sublime from the eighteenth century, like Dennis, Baillie and Addison.)[29] At the same time, in excluding art from his account of the sublime he also inadvertently touches on another important aspect of art in this context. It is Adorno who recognises this most clearly. Adorno writes:

> With profound justification Kant defined the concept of the sublime by the resistance of spirit to the overpowering. The feeling of the sublime does not correspond immediately with what appears; towering mountains are eloquent not as what crushes overwhelmingly but as images of a space liberated from fetters and strictures, a liberation in which it is possible to participate.[30]

This also relates to a further connection made by Adorno, raised in Part I. That is to say:

> The concept of nature held by the Enlightenment was partly responsible for the invasion of art by the Sublime. As the absolutist world of forms (which viewed nature as impetuous, crude and plebeian) began to

---

29. I am referring to the recent dissertation by Catharine Brillenburg Wurth, which explores these aspects in detail.
30. Adorno, *Aesthetic Theory*, p. 199.

be criticized, the practice of art underwent a radical change towards the end of the eighteenth century; it began to be infiltrated by the Sublime which Kant had considered to be an aspect of nature alone.[31]

Adorno suggests two things: (i) that the eighteenth-century Enlightenment period projected its fear of the elemental forces of society on to nature (this was just before the elemental upheaval of the French Revolution); and (ii) that the incorporation of the elemental into art, as the taboo, the ugly and the repulsive, also led to the emancipation of subjectivity in art and the move towards the autonomy of art works. The sublime becomes 'sublimated' within the structure of the autonomous work of art.

2. CONSTRUCTION OF THE SUBLIME

I shall now return to a consideration of Burke — himself later profoundly disturbed by the effects of the French Revolution, the experience of which can only have confirmed his theories of the sublime formulated over twenty years earlier — to elaborate on these ideas. First, there is the recognition that it is, above all, the calculated use of obscurity and darkness that is fundamental to the effect of the constructed sublime. Burke writes: "To make any thing very terrible, obscurity seems in general to be necessary."[32] He takes this further through an extended taxonomy of categories of the sublime, arguing — perhaps with more than a dash of irony — that words are most appropriate for the creation of obscurity, for their capacity to suggest horrors without giving clear form to them. He suggests that "it is one thing to make an idea clear, and another to make it *affecting* to the imagination. ... The proper manner of conveying the *affections* of the mind from one to another, is by words; there is a great insufficiency in all other methods of communication."[33] But then he goes on to argue the case for instrumental music as the extreme case that proves the rule — that obscurity can indeed be conjured up most effectively

---

31. Adorno, *Aesthetic Theory*, p. 280.
32. Burke, *A Philosophical Enquiry*, p. 54.
33. Burke, *A Philosophical Enquiry*, pp. 55–56.

without words, insisting that "so far is a clearness of imagery from being absolutely necessary to an influence upon the passions, that they may be considerably operated upon without presenting any image at all, by certain sounds adapted to that purpose; of which we have a sufficient proof in the acknowledged and powerful effects of instrumental music".[34] His conclusions are intriguing, and even paradoxical in their implications for the idea of what I am here calling the 'constructed sublime': "In reality a great clearness helps but little towards affecting the passions, as it is in some sort an enemy to all enthusiasms whatsoever."[35] In fact, the creation of obscurity in this sense certainly calls for a high degree of calculation, and even clarity, in that considerable technical means are needed to achieve it. This applies just as much to what could be called the 'popular' or 'vernacular sublime' — for example, Hammer horror films, or the remarkable technical and technological means on display in the *Lord of the Rings* trilogy of films, designed to construct an experience of the sublime on the grandest and most gothic scale — as it does to a work like Stockhausen's *Mantra* discussed earlier. I would like to explore these ideas a little further by taking a movement from Schoenberg's *Pierrot lunaire* — No. 8, 'Nacht' — as a case in point.

Schoenberg's Nightmare

Schoenberg's *Pierrot lunaire* (1912) has remarkable directness and immediacy at a gestural and expressive level, despite — or perhaps because of — the somewhat mannered and disturbing effect of the *Sprechstimme* (the half spoken, half sung voice part). And yet it is also a highly self-conscious and constructed work, its powerful and stifling sense of horror arising from the textural detail of its construction. The whole piece, as has often enough been pointed out, is a journey through madness and nightmare, characterized by a manic obsessiveness laced with brittle irony and humour, and an acute self-consciousness. One sign of its obsessiveness is the all-pervasive use of the numbers 3 and 7 — the work falls into three parts each of seven movements, adding up to 21 (2+1), and much

---

34. ibid.
35. ibid.

of the motivic material is dominated by three-note cells. The first part of the work is a kind of descent into the abyss, the second, which begins with 'Nacht' and ends with 'Enthauptung' ('Decapitation') is a dark night of claustrophobic horrors, and the third part, which begins with 'Heimweh' ('Homesickness'), is a transformative journey home, ending with the delicately nostalgic 'O alter Duft aus Märchenzeit' ('O ancient perfume from the age of fairy tales'). 'Nacht' comes therefore at the point of greatest concentration and stifled terror in the work. Giraud's poem is itself obsessively constructed, like all the others in the work, according to the same 13-line formula of three 'verses' making up the pattern of 4+4+5 lines with a rigid scheme of lines 1 and 2 recurring as lines 7 and 8, and line 13 being a repetition of line 1. The text describes huge black wings descending upon the sleeper to blot out the light of the sun, murdering memories and stifling breath in an extreme image of total suffocation, darkness, silence and standstill. Indeed, if a visual image were to be summoned by this piece, then it must surely be the famous Fuseli painting *The Nightmare*. This dates from the 1790s and exists in several versions. All show a woman lying across a bed in a room obscured by deep shadows out of which emerge terrifying visions — a fiery horse's head, and other shapes too unclear to make out. On her chest sits a dark goblin-like figure, a incubus, pressing with his weight the air from her body. Burke's own imagery can only amplify this, when he talks of "how greatly night adds to our dread, in all cases of danger, and how much the notions of ghosts and goblins, of which none can form clear ideas, affect minds, which give credit to the popular tales concerning such sorts of beings".[36]

'Nacht' itself falls into three sections, with the frenetic climax, a descent to the lowest regions of the piano, cello and bass clarinet and voice, coming just over half way through. The music is constructed entirely out of one three-note cell, E-G-E♭, the first three bars consisting of the densest possible set of permutations and superimpositions of this material in the lowest register of the piano, plus the motif appearing also between the cello and the bass

---

36. ibid.

Example 1: Schoenberg, *Pierrot lunaire*, No. 8, 'Nacht', first page of score.

clarinet. The three-note cell has as its continuation a seven-note chromatically descending scale, followed by a leap of an interval of a 7th (variable — sometimes a diminished 7th, sometimes a minor or a major 7th, but the gesture of a leap is always recognizable). These three elements — the cell, the chromatic scale and the leap — are almost immediately shown to be aspects of the same motif, in that the proto-chromatic scale is contained within the three notes, as is the leap of a 7th (i.e., by inverting the semitone step). In constructing the whole piece out of this material Schoenberg succeeds in creating the atmosphere of total suffocation as an unmistakable sonic image and as an exact complement to the text. What is disturbing about the piece (and in performance it comes across as one of the most powerful movements in the whole work) is the combination of visceral gestural image and the infinite detail and intricacy of that image. Density and obscurity are created through extreme precision of means.

Ferneyhough and the descent into the maelstrom

If one were to attempt to identify the central 'problem' around which most modernist art revolves — and this includes Brian Ferneyhough's music — it could be understood in purely structural, self-referential terms, and could be formulated as follows: to integrate conflicting levels in such a way as to retain and reveal the fractures which resist integration. The great tension generated by the attempt to contain powerful conflicting forces, and the inevitable failure to succeed in this, so that the fractures come to dominate the structures in a manner that creates a sense of dynamic and dramatic intensity and at the same time a fear that things will fall apart — all this creates an experience of the sublime. In Adorno's words:

> after the fall of formal beauty, the sublime was the only aesthetic idea left to modernism. ... The ascendancy of the sublime is one with art's compulsion that fundamental contradictions not be covered up but fought through in themselves; reconciliation for them is not the result of the conflict but exclusively that the conflict becomes eloquent.[37]

---

37. ibid., p. 197.

I have suggested elsewhere that Ferneyhough's compositions hang on the edge of chaos, and recall Edgar Alan Poe's short story *The Descent into the Maelstrom*: they create a kind of extreme order and focus which is at the same time shaped by the forces which surround and threaten its unity. The highly constructed character of Ferneyhough's music increases the sense of the sublime, in that the complexity of construction around vertiginous scenes of threatening chaos, recalls the source of much of Ferneyhough's inspiration — particularly in the cycle *Carceri d'invenzione*— in the drawings of Piranesi. Ferneyhough's music has a graphic and physical quality, calling up images of different levels and dimensions in dynamic interaction, bursting through, disappearing, reaching brief moments of equilibrium, collapsing, reassembling in new configurations. This experience of calculation in the face of chaos invokes Kant's 'mathematical sublime'. At the same time this situation has an inevitable element of the comical and the absurd which coexists with the experience of the sublime and is probably inseparable from it today. This was also noticed by Adorno:

> The legacy of the sublime is unassuaged negativity, as stark and illusionless as was once promised by the semblance of the sublime. This is however at the same time the legacy of the comic, which was always nourished by a feeling for the diminutive, the ludicrously pompous and insignificant, and which, for the most part, shored up established domination. The nonentity is comic by the claim to relevance that it registers by its mere existence and by which it takes the side of its opponent; once seen through, however, the opponent – power, grandeur – has itself become a nonentity. Tragedy and comedy perish in modern art and preserve themselves in it as perishing.[38]

IN CONCLUSION

The historical rise of the autonomous artwork, in freeing itself from direct social function, also led to possibilities for reflexion in musical terms within the sphere of the work—what Adorno referred to as a form of conceptless cognition. This process—

---

38. ibid., p. 199.

which is also one of increasing rationalization of musical structures — is at the same time a process of complexification. In one sense this reflects a social process of extreme rationalization, which stands over against us and, in Max Weber's terms, imprisons us in its 'iron cage' of proliferating systems of finance, administration and bureaucracy fundamental to modern capitalist society. Rationalization in the aesthetic sphere, on the other hand, operates as a kind of mimesis, or sublimation of the social process of ever-increasing rationalization. It is a form of rationalization and complexification with different ends; that is to say, aesthetic rationalization can act mimetically as a kind of protection against social (i.e. means-ends) rationalization. But this process also leads to an experience which has more in common with the experience of the sublime than with that of formal beauty, in the eighteenth-century sense of 'taste'. The complexification of the art work and the corresponding intensification of the aesthetic experience in terms of obscurity and unintelligibility — that is, the deliberate "production of things, we do not know what they are", to paraphrase Adorno in relation to Beckett — also leads back to an experience akin to that of the sublime in nature, but of nature as opposition to systematicity. In this context the concept of nature has an aspect of utopian promise, albeit unnamed, undefined. Interestingly, the concept of the sublime in relation to twentieth-century and contemporary music could therefore, in these terms, be understood to have returned to a concept of mimesis. But it is not that music *is* nature. It is through its extreme systematicity and constructedness that it comes close to nature, in the process preserving the idea of individual consciousness beyond social systematic constructedness.

I conclude with two thoughts. First Lyotard, in agreement with Adorno in this matter, says that "the system ... has the consequence of causing the forgetting of what escapes it".[39] Finally, Adorno, reconstituting nature as indeterminate promise, writes: "The identity of the artwork with the subject is as complete as the identity of nature with itself should some day be."[40]

---

39. Lyotard, 'Introduction: About the Human', in: *The Inhuman*, p. 2.
40. Adorno, *Aesthetic Theory*, p. 63.

BIBLIOGRAPHY

Adorno, T.W., *Ästhetische Theorie, Gesammelte Schriften 7*, ed. Rolf Tiedemann (Frankfurt/Main: Suhrkamp Verlag, 1970). English trans. as *Aesthetic Theory*, trans. Robert Hullot-Kentor (London: Athlone Press, 1997); also trans. Christian Lenhardt (London: Routledge, 1984).

—'Die Idee der Naturgeschichte' [1932], *Gesammelte Schriften I*, ed. Rolf Tiedemann (Frankfurt/Main: Suhrkamp Verlag, 1973), pp. 325-344. Trans. as 'The Idea of Natural-History', trans. Robert Hullot-Kentor, in *Telos* 60 (Summer 1984), pp. 111-124.

Brillenburg Wurth, Catharina, *The Musically Sublime: Infinity, Indeterminacy, Irresolvability* (Doctoral dissertation: Rijksuniversiteit Groningen, 2002).

Burke, Edmund, *A Philosophical Enquiry into the Origin of our Ideas of the Sublime and the Beautiful* (1757) (Oxford: OUP, 1990).

Cage, John, *Silence* (London: Marion Boyars, 1968).

Collingwood, R.G., *The Idea of Nature* (Oxford: Clarendon Press, 1945).

Darwin, Charles, *The Expression of the Emotions in Man and Animals*, Introduction, Afterword and Commentaries by Paul Ekman (London: Harper Collins, 1998; orig. John Murray, 1872).

Hindemith, Paul, *The Craft of Musical Composition* (1937), Bk.I, trans. Arthur Mendel (London/Mainz/New York: Schott/Associated Music Publishers, 1942).

Kant, Immanuel, *Critique of Judgment* (1790), trans. Werner S. Pluhar (Indianapolis: Hackett, 1983).

Lukács, Georg, *History and Class Consciousness* (1922), trans. Rodney Livingstone (London: Merlin Press, 1971).

Lyotard, Jean-François, *Leçons sur l'analytique du sublime* (Paris: Editions Galilée, 1991). Trans. as *Lessons on the Analytic of the Sublime*, trans. Elizabeth Rottenberg (Stanford: Stanford University Press, 1994).

—*L'Inhumain: Causeries sur le temps* (Paris: Editions Galilée, 1988). Trans. as *The Inhuman: Reflections on Time*, trans. Geoffrey Bennington and Rachel Bowlby (Cambridge: Polity Press, 1991).

Meyer, Leonard B., *The Spheres of Music: A Gathering of Essays* (Chicago & London: University of Chicago Press, 2000).

Motte-Haber, Helga de la, *Musik und Natur: Naturanschauung und musikalische Poetik* (Laaber: Laaber Verlag, 2000).

Paddison, Max, *Adorno's Aesthetics of Music* (Cambridge: Cambridge University Press, 1993).

—*Adorno, Modernism and Mass Culture* (London: Kahn & Averill, 1996; rev. edition 2004).

—'Postmodernisme et la survie de l'avant-garde', in Irène Deliège and Max Paddison (eds.), *Musique contemporaine: Perspectives théoriques et philosophiques* (Liège: Mardaga, 2001), pp. 249-266.

—Review: 'Leonard B. Meyer, *The Spheres of Music*', *Musicae Scientiae* Vol. VI, No. 2 (Fall 2002), pp. 279-86.

Schleuning, Peter, *Die Sprache der Natur in der Musik des 18. Jahrhunderts* (Stuttgart: Metzler, 1999).

Schoenberg, Arnold, *Theory of Harmony* (1911), trans. Roy E. Carter (London: Faber, 1978).

Spencer, Herbert, "The Origin and Function of Music" (1857), in: *Literary Style and Music* (New York: Philosophical Library, 1951), pp. 45-106.

MUSIC AND POLITICS
Konrad Boehmer

When in the 1960s my generation began to consider the relation between music and politics, the Vietnam war, started by the US administration under a threadbare pretext (Maddox / Gulf of Tonkin incident, 2 August 1964), was still raging. This war, whose barbaric frenzy and napalm devastations had seen no equal since the second World War, shocked our then young generation in two respects. Firstly, we could not comprehend how a nation which had liberated us twenty years previously from the horrors of the Nazi reign of terror could now be guilty of comparable crimes. Secondly we were shocked by the fact that all western European governments supported the USA with the slavish loyalty of vassals. Also, the appeasement policy of the Soviet Union caused us to doubt its endless world-peace rituals: this political entity would sell the most expensive and advanced weapons to such nations as Egypt at the drop of a hat, while refusing them to Vietnam, which desperately needed such things. It was staggering to see how quickly liberators would mutate into perpetrators of genocide, and state capitalists into social imperialists.

Those composers whose dismay caused their ink to freeze on the paper belonged to a generation which had grown up in the traditions of serial or (American) chance-derived music. They had observed how both traditions, already in the 1960s, had manoeuvred themselves into the impasse of an 'aleatoric' or 'graphic' music, from which they could only escape by completely relinquishing their aesthetic ideals, by adapting themselves step by step to traditional bourgeois standards. For the first time, the idea came to these composers that the aesthetic foundations of the radical postwar music could as such become biased by the paradigms of bourgeois thinking, especially that of an 'autonomous' music as had arisen since Hanslick, albeit under the derisive laughter of the then important composers. The total de-functionalisation exemplified in Hanslick's 'sounding moving forms' had already become a rearguard action in the 19th century, within a bourgeois society which was on its way to subjecting *all* areas of life to the principle of maximising profit, thus depriving them of their intrinsic meaning. At that point it seemed that the only way out for an advanced art music wishing to evade mundane influences was just such an abstract floating in a no less abstract heavenly abode of ideas.

Thus we found ourselves in a twofold dilemma: the social relapse into pure barbarity left no concrete future perspectives, and the music had manoeuvred itself into a niche on the periphery of society, from which it (or rather its composers) could only squawk to the world like a parrot behind the bars of its cage. It seemed as if Raymond Radiguet's words had finally become completely true: "L'avant-garde commence debout et elle finit à genoux".

Those who at that time were in their twenties had grown up in a postwar world of petty-bourgeois restoration, touched only marginally by Anglo-American pop culture, whose development into the globally dominant cultural norm of a dynamic capitalist restoration nobody could yet foresee. Into a culture, moreover, whose apparent potential for protest would be converted with lightning speed into an instrument of social pacification and control of the young generation. And this in the interest of all those who were striving in Vietnam to make their modern, technologically perfected barbarism presentable in genteel company. There seemed to be no exit by musical means from such a world of total encirclement, and it is embarrassing to this day to read the utterances of (already established) composers of that period, as they tried to install themselves in it. They seemed only to confirm a general feeling of failure.

Many a composer of the young generation had read Adorno or even a little Bloch, and Marcuse's One-Dimensional Man seemed to be the confirmation of the hopelessness we all felt. At the time I attempted to express that general feeling in an extensive text entitled "Revolution of Music or Music of Revolution?".[1] Anyhow, the attitude of the Frankfurt School—and especially Adorno—

---

1. Konrad Boehmer, "Revolution der Musik oder Musik der Revolution?", in: *The World of Music* vol.1, pp. 19-33 (abridged versions in German, French and English of the original Dutch in: *Raster* 1969/4, pp. 539-60).

seemed suspect to us, having abandoned the working class as subject of revolution already in the 1930s, and beginning to consider society merely as an intangible totality whose subjects were just as 'dehumanised' as social structures themselves, rather than searching out the first seeds of new subjects of social transformation. More recently, André Gorz has aptly analysed this about-face towards a negative idealism.[2] In the end, none of these writings offered any perspective whatsoever for actual musical activity, as was also the case with those few writings of Marx which were accessible at that time, for example the early writings or the *Outlines of a Critique of Political Economy*. Even the Communist Manifesto, while predicting the process of decay of bourgeois culture, gave no instructions for its concrete overthrow, which indeed is impossible within the system of bourgeois norms. Around 1968 — the year of the great rebellion — there were some young composers who agreed quickly with the young student-revolutionaries that the perspectives of a truly new music could only be formulated after a comprehensive social revolution. Much evidence still favours this interpretation, only the notion of revolution has changed in the meantime. It has become more dialectical and less romantic.

Just like the rebellious students, the composers at that time also found themselves in a no-man's-land, in which they saw only raging fires rather than their own historical perspectives. Around 1968 we began to discover Hanns Eisler, and with him the theory and practice of the worker's music movement of the 1920s, of which he is still rightly regarded as the most important theoretician. In western Europe it was almost impossible to obtain Eisler's writings, so that we had to content ourselves with those fragments which had been published in the GDR. These were far from giving us any insight into the 'whole' Eisler, in his dialectical attitude towards the dramatically changing periods leading from the Weimar Republic to the rise of fascism, and from the time of his emigration to that of the GDR. We perceived only the Eisler of direct class-struggle from the time of the Weimar KPD (German

---

2. André Gorz, *Arbeit zwischen Misere und Utopie*, Frankfurt/Main 2000, p. 181ff.

Communist Party), and it was exactly this reading which confirmed our conception of a music which only after the radical overthrow of society would be able to redevelop perspectives for the future. This conception was too short-sighted, but even today it seems to me not completely mistaken.

While the most radical students of '1968' and also some few composers and other artists busied themselves with building up social-revolutionary and communist parties, which for their part awaited the emergence of the proletarian revolutionary subject (and which were overjoyed when a real worker happened to stray into their party offices), a radical recomposition of capital was taking place almost invisibly, based upon the development of new digital technology which to this day makes possible its global expansion: we sang the Internationale and failed to notice that under our very eyes a completely different International was emerging: that of 'informational' capitalism. The contradiction between these two contrary movements called forth direct consequences on the level of culture. While the young composers intended to develop a music which would be useful to the expected revolutionary upheaval, and thus held conservatively to the historic models of the 1920s workers' movement, the culture industry appropriated the term 'revolution' for its own dynamic, which articulated itself in wave after wave of fashionable products, whose use-value became increasingly limited and whose shelf-life accordingly became ever shorter: the acquisition of cultural products became an end in itself, leading finally to that form of commodity fetishism which today completely dominates youth culture. The nature of this fetishism is based — as Gerhard Scheit has formulated it — on the consumption of "the reification of interpersonal relations, and actually of the personal itself".[3] The about-turn from manufacturing to service industry, as it outlined itself at the time, was based on the development of technologies which are equally suitable both for production and for distribution, and which have themselves become a fetish-object in the meantime.

---

3. Gerhard Scheit, "Vielerlei Gebrauchswert", in: *Mülltrennung. Beiträge zu Politik, Literatur und Musik*, Hamburg 1998, p. 50.

From a musical point of view, there began after about 1970 that tendency which would subsequently begin to dominate the whole of culture, namely that turn towards postmodern indifference which has now been elevated to the rank of fashion-philosophy, where previously one would simply have spoken of cultural eclecticism. My colleague Tristan Murail has classed this kind of salon philosophy with 'economic neoliberalism', to which postmodernity is "linked in a subtle and pernicious manner".[4] What was once called 'new music' became split into fashions which have succeeded one another with increasing rapidity, and which step by step exploit all the arsenals of past musical languages and shamelessly show off the trophies. In the meantime, there are for example composers in Holland selling in the media the most schoolboy-like Palestrina counterpoint, whose notes they stretch to 'new age' lengths, as the redemption from all the evils of New Music.[5] Even the music in whose revolutionary effect we once trusted has been sucked into this vortex of the culture industry: the Eisler which could be separated and degraded as cabaret was rendered harmless, while the other Eisler was not performed at all.

Amongst the composers of my generation it was in the first instance Christian Wolff, Cornelius Cardew, Frederic Rzewski and myself who at least made the attempt to revolutionise music, and thus to break out of the ivory tower of pseudo-autonomy. The total failure of this attempt deserves attention. Where we integrated songs from the workers' movement or from revolutionary liberation movements into works for concert use, they were received by the public as though they were materials from the classical-romantic repertoire. Cornelius Cardew tried for a while to bring revolutionary content to the music of a folk-pop group he had formed, the result being no more than rather mediocre polit-rock. Finally he manoeuvred himself into a totally insoluble contradiction. His *Thälmann Variations* are based on a workers'

---

4. Tristan Murail, "Entretien" (interview with Pierre Michel) in: Peter Szendy, *Tristan Murail*, Paris 2002, p. 53.
5. The composers Franssens, Borstlap and Hamburg proudly call themselves 'Composers' Group Amsterdam'.

song from the Weimar Republic, which becomes the theme for a series of variations in 'biedermeier'-romantic style, failing by far to match the compositional standards of Mendelssohn or Schumann. Given that the melody is already impoverished and sketchy, the attempt was in every respect tragic, and proved that without a revolutionary subject there can be no revolutionary music. During the 1970s I had many bitter disagreements, especially with my friend Cardew, which caused the parting of our political — not personal! — ways. Cardew was unable to confess to any kind of failure, and isolated himself in a tiny Marxist-Leninist party which primarily supported the isolationist politics of the Albanian leader Enver Hoxha. Nevertheless, in our critical attitude towards the Germanic-reactionary ideologies of Stockhausen we were of one mind to the very end.

During those years, even the exponents of what we described as 'bourgeois music' adopted increasingly radical positions, aimed at condemning any kind of musical structure or architectonics, in short, any kind of coherence, as 'ideology' or 'false consciousness'. This attitude, which might be considered the last flower on the tree of musical 'autonomy', tends towards the abolition of music as such, and internalises in a highly ideological manner the positions adopted by Cage in for example *4'33"* or *Variations I*. A critique of ideology which in its solipsism no longer perceives the dynamic of reality tends all too quickly to become itself an ideology. Since the 1970s numerous composers have been augmenting forms of musical complexity (in Germany even the idiotic term 'complexism' is currently doing the rounds), which sometimes have quite fascinating moments, but which are completely unfit for any kind of aesthetic positioning with regard to social criticism: nonuplets, within which septuplets are hiding and behind which quintuplets are peeping out, renounce any relationship to musical time just as Bits and Bytes do to lived time. Where complexity is no longer the basis of the creation of musical meaning, but has become in itself the goal of musical structuring, it stumbles precisely into the trap of those forms of failed social enlightenment, whose 'negative' dialectic Adorno once emphasised in the notion of freedom of the classical Enlightenment: it "acts against the old oppression and advances the new one, which itself remains stuck in the principle of rationality".[6] Those forms of new music which appeal to this principle with a positivist coolness are exactly what Adorno sees as 'totalitarian'. It can be considered as the 'negative dialectics' of these forms of music which internalise a principle of increasing interdependence and unfreedom, having at the same moment the pretention of being able from this position to unfold the potential of social liberation, as from a lofty perch on horseback. Small wonder that those graphical composition-sketches so beloved of musicologists look confusingly like diagrams of exchange rates: both cases are ruled by a pious belief in parameters, which are applied as determinative values without a thought as to what is being determined. This similarity touches the essence of the problem: the scientific discipline of acoustics cares as little for the (human) field of perception as do the 'benchmarks' of the international exchange business for the unemployed of Rabat, Dortmund or Liverpool. While 'material' began already in the hands of the 'Vienna School' to dissolve from the composition process, becoming instead the object of idiosyncratic organisational techniques, these very techniques began from 1950 onwards to replace the composition process. To the same extent that exchange rate data are no longer linked to concrete use values, but only to the fiction of 'shareholder value', the parameter values of 'complex' music are no longer founded in the perceptual qualities of sounds or structures but only in the concept of a schematic numerical 'correctness'. "That which is correct", as Herbert Brün once said, "is nowhere near important". Just as the musical ideology of complexity reflects the structure of the currently dominant social order, commercial music expresses its ideology, its naïve and cynical self-image. For this reason, neither of these musical spheres offers a real aesthetic alternative, since neither comes near to making contact with the essence of these ruling circumstances, still less expressing them. With respect to this essence, anti-war cantatas and cluster-laden memorials to Hiroshima are nothing more than poster art, which hold on to a symptom without in any way revealing an essence.

---

6. T.W. Adorno, *Negative Dialektik*, Frankfurt/Main 1966, p. 211.

Let there be no misunderstanding: the way out of current aesthetic aporias consists in no way of a return to Rousseau's 'back to nature' call, which indeed — similarly to Heidegger — sees the historical process exclusively as a process of decline. Rousseau even saw the primacy of harmony — which he himself maintained — as a degeneration, without noticing the extent to which his own reduction of musical structure to a rural idyll was a totally anachronistic historical construct.[7] Such constructs point at best to symptoms of social unease, while remaining unable in the least to clarify their origins. Similar forms of historic reductionism and yearning for a 'return' to what is pure, true and 'human' have become once again common currency in our time. So far as they polemicise against 'the' serial music, they all miss their objective, which they declare to be absolute without in any way getting its sociohistorical implications in their sights. There exists no time in which either the world or music would have been 'in order'. In such a case humanity would have been 'finished', 'accomplished'. More convincing is Ernst Bloch's argument: "I am. But I don't own myself. That is why we come into being."[8] This goes for composers too.

Let us return to the consequences of the year 1968. I have already mentioned that the young composers of the time also dedicated themselves to a historical reductionism: they dreamt so to speak of invoking a working class, by reconstructing a proletarian music of struggle from the interwar period, which they needed in order to be able to carry through their desired revolution. Thus an attempt was made to 'compose' the revolutionary subject, while forgetting the social reality in relation to which music must define itself, however utopian its aspirations. The fact that working-class youth

---

7. Jean-Jacques Rousseau, *Ecrits sur la musique*, Paris 1979, p. 248: "Voilà comment le chant devient, par degrés, un art entièrement séparé de la parole, dont il tire son origine; comment les harmoniques des sons firent oublier les inflexions de la voix; et comment enfin, borné à l'effet purement physique du concours des vibrations, la musique se trouva privée des effets moraux qu'elle avoit produits quand elle étoit doublement la voix de la nature". Vincenzo Galilei had argued similarly against mediaeval polyphony, 200 years before Rousseau, except that for him harmony was exactly the means by which song could be liberated…

8. Ernst Bloch, *Spuren*, Frankfurt/Main 1959, p. 7.

in 1968 favoured *Street Fightin' Man* and had never come across the name of Nono was a first signal for the approaching period in which the new capitalism took for itself the term 'revolution' — also from a cultural point of view — and the classical proletariat was bit by bit pulverised into 'Woodstockers'.

This capitalist 'revolution' was completely underestimated by the self-elected young revolutionaries. While regarding the victory of the tiny Vietnamese nation against the gigantic war machine of American imperialism as the upbeat to a world revolution, they completely overlooked the fact that, in the background, a push towards rationalisation was taking place whose material foundations lay in exactly that military technology whose grotesque face we had seen grinning in Vietnam. This historic change consisted broadly of a shift from mechanical, 'analogue' modes of production to digital ones. Since the end of the 18th century, one of the most radical upheavals in human history had taken place, with mechanical-industrial production at its base, whose structure depended upon those forms of industrial and financial capitalism which Marx so mercilessly laid bare. Towards the beginning of the 20th century, this system found its apex in the brutal production methods of Fordism and Taylorism, in which human beings became no more than dispensable extensions of machines. After both world wars had been concluded in favour of the most advanced nation in terms of productivity (the USA), those methods of production had a tendency to slide towards crisis, from which such nations as Japan profited by the introduction of completely new ('Toyotist') methods of production, which were much more flexible. The western industrial countries then applied themselves with some urgency to the rationalisation of production by means of digital technology. Until the present, these techniques have been perfected to such a degree that they have developed into an end in themselves, which overshoots any possible use-value.

This revolution generated in the first instance the sort of ideology of 'freedom from labour', and of a society made 'feasible' entirely on the basis of rational technology, which has been constantly been repeated since the 1950s. New products and objects for use have increasingly become adapted to these ideological topoi. Although we have known for decades that this gigantic wave of innovation is devoid of any valuation of its (technological) consequences[9] (for example we know how carcinogenic the effects of 'gene-therapy' can be[10]), it rolls inexorably over us in search of the realisation of those aims which André Gorz has recently described as the "total victory of dematerialised capital."[11] For half a century, the slogan which triumphantly accompanies these developments goes under the name of freedom. But this notion, which had emerged at a central moment in the Enlightenment, has in more recent history become perverted into its opposite. This is inherent to the quality of the technological revolution: where production in the first industrial revolution aimed chiefly at the means of production and use-values, the second industrial revolution produces the producer himself, along with his entire living environment. Those who could during the bourgeois era feel themselves at least a subject confronting a world of objects, are nowadays the product of the 'new economy' and the 'I-society', which dictate their patterns of behaviour so precisely that each individual is reduced to acting out whatever those standardised patterns tell him to be. This dictatorship neither intrudes from without nor rules 'over' the individual: it is represented in all individuals. On this coincidence is founded the ideology of 'freedom' in the western industrial states: happy slaves…

How things could arrive at this point can be described here only in rough outlines. With capitalist-industrial production, an exchange value is slipped over the pure use-value of consumer goods, which — with increasing mass-production — must go on being realised even when there is no need for their direct use-value. For this reason, a 'commodity aesthetic' already developed in the 19th century, lending products an aesthetic flair which had nothing to do with their use-value. Already during the final decades of that century, this aestheticised world of commodities entered the magical advertising world, which for its part fed with increasing greed off the visual arts and subsequently music as well.

---

9. See Jedediah Purdy, *Das Elend der Ironie*, Hamburg 2002, p. 166 (German translation of *For Common Things*, New York 1999).
10. See "Krank geheilte Kinder" in: *Der Spiegel* no. 7, 20/2/2003, p. 140ff.
11. André Gorz, *loc.cit.*, p. 164.

Just as from the end of the 19th century 'electricity' as a new productive force enables the reproduction of reproductions (also in music), so the digital economy strives to a reproduction of the appearance of the world of commodities. It does so in such a way that the use-value — which is the relation between the individual and the outside world — disappears completely behind the 'experience' of that appearance. The mass markets of the 'new economy' make profits of billions with products which are not products at all, but which in the form of 'entertainment' occupy all the psychic spaces, the entire 'Begehrungsvermögen' ('capacity to desire' — Immanuel Kant) of the social subjects. This is the material essence of the 'virtual reality' which nevertheless encircles us in a very real way.

Something of this totalising momentum exists already within digital technology itself. It is designed not only for limitless reproduction, and infinite recycling of that which is reproduced, but also for all-embracing social interdependence. In our passports we already find a code number which renders us totally open to the inspection of the authorities, and our private e-mail addresses are immediately known to all commercial companies, who incidentally already know our credit card data and buying habits. The state apparatuses dream of a 'transparent man' and geneticists in any case want to replace us by our replicas, in short: digital capitalism requires a comprehensive knowledge of our most secret movements in order to bring them into tune with its products. Whereas we identify phases of technological innovation of past times with the 'progress' of civilisation, the present all-permeating technological revolution tends towards total paralysis, because from the outset it channels any free thought and action into its self-designed structures. If, however, this were all true, then the cultural analyses of 'critical theory' would be correct, and we would indeed be dealing with a monolithic, self-perpetuating system. But even this 'brave new world' has its contradictory material substrates, whose consequence consists in the fact that the increasing automatising of all domains of life also encompasses those of production. Labour invested in the new economy liquidates labour itself, whose social significance is in any case hardly clear to us any more. But that liquidation of labour liquidates with it the potential consumer. What was once the classical capitalist cycle of crises condenses increasingly into a permanent crisis. This crisis is goaded on still further by that of the financial markets, which have disengaged themselves completely from the level of production and which drive an entire country (Argentina) to bankruptcy today, in order to destroy the currency of another (Thailand) tomorrow. This so-called 'globalisation' reminds us all too clearly of the robber barons of previous ages, defying any kind of state order. Worse still: where gigantic riches are allowed to accumulate precisely through the liquidation of labour, man indeed runs the risk of becoming a "superfluous factory product of nature", in Schopenhauer's mocking words.

We find ourselves therefore not just in an economic but in a historical crisis, from which no traditional recipe can help us to escape: incurable unemployment in the industrial world, renewed slavery in the countries of cheap labour and at the same time a shameless exploitation of their natural resources, which drives the bank accounts of the 'global players' to hitherto unknown heights. A world in which — as Viviane Forrester has formulated it — "the proletariat, or what remains of it, fights to win back its inhuman [labour] conditions" and "the future is designed for our superfluity".[12] It would involve great skill to translate into something qualitatively new these contemporary forms of total social interdependence, which are nothing other than a derivative of the worldwide entanglement of capital; something which I at least can imagine only as socialistic: a sensible re-establishment of use-value for the benefit of all. How the arts, and especially music, can orient themselves in relation to this crisis, is completely unclear. Yet one thing is clear: the disastrous revolution of which I have here given an outline is not a short-term process; it is a long-term evolution which will only reach its limits — passing beyond parties and governments — if its own internal conditions allow it to do so. But then it might already be too late. It is above all the invisibility of the structures of this revolution which makes taking a political-artistic standpoint in relation to it so difficult. We are

---

12. Viviane Forrester, *L'Horreur économique*, quoted from the Dutch edition, *De Terreur van de economie*, Amsterdam 1997, p. 127 and 159.

not the first to face such a situation. Beethoven, as a composer of daily politics, already showed a profound naivety in his obsession with Napoleon, or his repellent princely cantata (*Der glorreiche Augenblick*). Nevertheless he understood better than anyone, in his middle period, how to lend artistic expression to the revolutionary impetus of the bourgeois class. Our business, however, is to shed some light on music in its contemporary social position.

I have already pointed out that all musical genres — consciously or not — are closely interwoven with the social system I have just outlined. Regarding commercial genres there is little I need to tell you: they have, in the form of 'jingles', videos and ring tones, reduced music to fragments of sound, which satisfy the unremitting musical addiction of those who otherwise have no idea of how to fill up their emptied-out ego. This acoustical garbage heap has already generated billions in turnover. On the other hand, art music has always had a hard time in relation to the manifold forms of popular music. In relation to the new forms of commercial music it has shrunk almost to zero. Economically speaking it is non-existent, and in the media it is marginalised into unrecognisability. Its total disappearance is quite conceivable: the Roman Empire managed very well without any art music, and the situation in the USA is no different. Typical for all current forms of commercial music is that they are completely circumscribed by the norms of digital capitalism, as far as their modes of production and economic function are concerned, as well as their function within the machinery of society. This music offers immediate satisfaction of desire, and its hedonism guarantees that this addiction to satisfaction is prolonged indefinitely. Against the capitalist absorption of almost all music stands only a tiny island of truly creative production, which does not bow to the ruling norms. A purely economic comparison of both music worlds would not progress very far, since the production of art music evades any economic category: "creative labour cannot be socialised or codified"[13].

So it seems at least, although here too the reality is otherwise. The all-embracing social interdependence has already begun to

---

13. André Gorz, *loc.cit.*, p. 12.

gnaw at the edges of that little island of art music, the majority of whose composers it has succeeded in integrating within its social network. Until about 1950, new music resisted all the seductions of the capitalist culture industry — think of Schoenberg, Varèse or Webern — resulting in a difficult life for numerous composers, for the price of artistic independence increases by the day.

After the second World War — helped along by the bad conscience of various politicians — a process of socialisation has been imposed on the new music, which could be considered as a premonition of its being rendered totally superfluous. Already during the serial era, summer courses and epidemically-spreading composition classes at conservatories did their best to curtail the high-altitude flight of the avant-garde and subject it to the yoke of academicism. That was a risky business: the social need for that music was limited, and to this day no social desire for academic modernity has been observed. It is astonishing that the composers of the first postwar generation are even now — half a century later — considered to be the innovators, while the youngest generation of composers, from whom one might expect a breath of passion, are at most tolerated as a fleeting utility product. This looks damnably like the psychology of the commercial music market, which erects monuments to its founding fathers (Presley, Lennon, Jagger etc.) and recycles them through endless remakes, while their younger colleagues, as like one another as two peas, are retailed by MTV and similar trashy networks.

During the past half-century, a process already analysed by Pierre Bourdieu in connection with literary trends of the 19th century has unfolded on the terrain of art music. It is a process of shrinkage into a small field whose "principal function, however this may continue to be ignored", consists in "being its own market".[14] During the period of the 'bohemians' (between Baudelaire and Rimbaud) such tiny fields of art still stood in complete opposition to the bourgeoisie, and this opposition found its expression in the works themselves. That was the only political 'explosive' they had. In the music of the twentieth century, such fields have

---

14. Pierre Bourdieu, *Die Regeln der Kunst*, Frankfurt/Main 1999, p. 99 (German translation of *Les Règles de l'art*, Paris 1992).

multiplied, and have battled against one another more fiercely in the same measure as the middle class of society has seemed no longer to notice them. In western Europe since about 1950, there have arisen such structures as can even integrate artistic fields within a framework of state subvention measures, from which those fields have not to this day been able to liberate themselves. Since the entire production of art music is based on a pseudo-economy (because there is no way to find a relation between value and price), those state measures have imposed norms on musical production which it has in the meantime completely internalised, and this at the cost of artistic independence. In the Netherlands, for example, most composers are in point of fact already petty civil servants. If all those aforementioned measures had the effect of broadening the field, one could perhaps find cause to rejoice. The opposite is the case. The field becomes ever smaller, and has become internally differentiated to the point of atomisation: competitions, composers' workshops, foundations, commission subsidies, CDs, performances, postgraduate studies, composers' meetings and discussion groups, and as a recent innovation the way in which one venue after another pumps out whichever 'young composer' as if this had anything to do with aesthetic criteria. The newest fashion is that kind of young composer who does not really wish to be a composer at all, but who hastens from course to study, from study to workshop, and in so doing becomes an incarnation of that entire apparatus which is suffocating us. All of these measures, and many, many more, have resulted in an administrative structure which has developed a bureaucratic dynamic all of its own, and which must continually generate new projects in order to be able to legitimise itself, and the streams of subsidy which flow into it. This vault, which exercises a heavy pressure on free musical production, has in the course of recent decades delivered myriads of composers who produce nothing more than what they have heard from their composition teachers: pseudo-modern craftsmanship, with which they travel around like hawkers. The consequence of this nationalisation is not the survival of modern art music but the production of composers, who themselves become the means of legitimation of the state machinery. This means of legitimation is of course compelled to produce, in order to preserve his own personal subsidy-donations and thus to earn his living. Such an artificially-produced excess results mostly tragically in a single performance or in the filing cabinets of some institution. The parcelling-out of the field has the effect, among others, of producing a concentration on chamber music (most orchestras avoid modern music), which is a sociological anachronism. Radio stations are neither able to absorb all this production nor to integrate it within their increasingly commercial strategies: new music programmes are melting away like April snow. The concert halls are mostly empty and the increasing marginalisation of new music forces especially the younger composers into the most diverse forms of functionalisation, which in turn are taken up by the art-functionaries to conceive concerts in advance as 'events' which must then be supplied with 'content' by composers.

Since music for around a hundred years no longer has coherent structures at its disposal, its refunctionalisation, in point of fact its preparation for whatever heterogeneous aims may be imposed on it, is not such a difficult matter. To the 'jingles' or 'ringtones' of commercial music, art music answers with 'sound installations', 'electroclips' or similar rubbish. But even this functionalisation no longer functions: it takes place in social obscurity. In a nutshell: to the extent that the music, enclosed within the world of information technology, has abandoned its comprehension of the world, it takes flight into forms of presentation which renew themselves like fashions of the season. Whoever abandons substance can only retreat into pure appearance. From this point of view, contemporary art music draws ominously close to the normative structures of commercial music. It culminates in 'experiences', which in the end are the mimesis of events and situations exemplified in the media. What we actually observe in the historic aftermath of art music is close to what Manuel Castells has stated for the 'information society' in general: "the stream of spaces dissolves (...) time by disorganising the succession of events, by rendering them simultaneous and so installing society in an eternal present".[15]

---

15. Manuel Castells, *Die Netzwerkgesellschaft: Das Informationszeitalter I*, Opladen 2001, p. 523 (German translation of *The Rise of the Network Society: The Information Age I*, Oxford 1996).

Exactly this is the essence of that postmodernity which in commercial form "expresses the newly dominating ideology in a direct way".[16]

Whichever perspective one cares to take of the 'field', it suffers under a tragic contradiction: the increasing socialisation of ever more 'integrated' composers confronts a complete lack of social interest, and this in turn forces the composers to further increase their adaptation to the aforementioned state structures. They obey the demands placed on them, as do all other social minorities which are dependent on state subsidies. To the extent that composers are compelled to adapt to the new order, they are also compelled to participate actively in the self-destruction of art music by means of a total erosion of its substance. This process can be prevented by succeeding in the transformation of the social process itself. One thing is in any case certain: neither left-wing cantatas nor socialist oratorios have the ability to make any contribution here, and the anti-war songs are already being delivered by pop composers. In the face of the manifest political cruelties of our time, composers should take a stand as citizens with a conscience, rather than believing that string quartets or computer music will make any difference. The politicisation of music in the 19th and 20th centuries had the advantage of being able to turn itself against personalisations of power, which at the time had some point. Since, in the industrialised countries, the governments themselves are now no more than bookkeepers of economic compulsions imposed upon them by digi-capitalism, any personalised aesthetic protest has become a hollow gesture. The structures themselves, even though we can of course perceive people at their periphery, are invisible: that is their essence and their power. They cannot be handled in compositional/political terms by being captured in images. The idea of replicating them in musical structures belongs to the same kind of self-deception with which the avant-garde has for decades increasingly buried itself in obscurantism.

Hanns Eisler, who warned us many years ago about the "devastations wreaked by late capitalism in the minds of young

---

16. Castells, *loc.cit.*, p. 474.

composers"[17], repeatedly quoted the ancient Chinese philosopher Me-Ti: "The fact that people pursue music has four disadvantages: the hungry are not fed, the freezing are not warmed, the homeless remain homeless and the desperate remain unconsoled."[18] Eisler wanted to change the final phrase to "the desperate will be consoled", above all because of the advance of stupidity in music. Anyhow, I do not see putting any particular symbols into the world as possible political perspectives; I only see the absolute necessity for composers on the one hand to form broad coalitions against institutionally-promoted stupidity in music (and by thus against modern music industry), and on the other to take note of the fact that all the technological paradigms which they themselves have disseminated over the last fifty years have only driven them ever deeper into the Moloch of those technologically-based power structures which we should be fighting against. It is not a matter of thinking just about the quality of the musical products, but first and foremost about the quality of the modalities of production themselves. In the final analysis this means not to compose political music, but to compose music politically. As in every other social field, so also is the field of contemporary art music infused with politics even to its most sublime ramifications. The socially aware composer sees himself always confronted with the necessity of a double strategy: the intrastructural tendencies of his work also contribute to the transformation of the field. But not, in any case, if one merely designs actions that treat this field as if it were a circus ring. Such philosophically-garnished neo-Dada has degenerated into pure routine over the past forty years. The transformation of the field can only be achieved through transformation of the deep musical structure as well as the narrative structures; anything else is a Punch and Judy show for infantile adults. Such a (field-)transformation has no effect in and of itself, and cannot be more than a part — admittedly an aesthetically important part — of a much more far-reaching social transformation. Precisely here lies a not inconsiderable political responsibility for composers: however limited the direct effect of their aesthetic

---

17. Hanns Eisler, *Materialien zu einer Dialektik der Musik*, Leipzig 1973, p. 326.
18. Eisler, *loc.cit.*, p. 271/2.

decisions might be, they nonetheless bear this responsibility, whether their field contributes to the strengthening of the currently dominant neo-capitalist structures or to their erosion and final overthrow. All of this only makes sense when the music at least speaks to those people who in their own worlds are equally advocates of far-reaching social transformation. By once more stirring the sewage of postmodern décomposition, new music merely plays along with that kind of neo-liberalism whose henchman is neo-structuralist philosophy.

I cannot at this point formulate more than these perspectives. In any case there are no recipes. Perhaps, after all, a little more direct social engagement could bring some composers to ideas which cannot be delivered by the suffocating narrowness of the contemporary music world. How did Bertolt Brecht formulate it? "Sink into the filth, embrace the slaughterers, but change the world, it needs changing."[19] Whoever wishes to break out of the ivory tower of self-created illusions must forge his own crowbar.

---

19. Quoted from the setting by Hanns Eisler, in Eisler, *Lieder und Kantaten* vol.2, Leipzig 1957, p. 2.

TOWARDS A TERZA PRATTICA

Konrad Boehmer

Surely the most far-reaching paradigm shift in European music, occurring around a thousand years ago, is what Denis Stevens has called 'the transformation of sounds into symbols'[1]. This most radical revolution in western music history took place against the background of a profound social transformation generally known as the 'Carolingian Renaissance', a term I regard as seriously wide of the mark. Nothing in fact was 'reborn', and Charlemagne behaved in truth more as a brigand and mass murderer than as a man of culture. In his book *Geschichte als Weg zum Musikverständnis*[2], Georg Knepler has extensively analysed the repercussions of this social change on the forms of musical thought and production, as well as the rise of the composer as a new representative of these new forms. Furthermore, Knepler has analysed this process not within the conventional framework of history as 'result' but of history as a complex of problems, attempting to lay bare the processes of thinking and learning. The development of an analytical notation divided the flow of a melody into indivisible steps, as in differential geometry, thus bringing the single note within the grasp of composition. The fixation of a flow of sound by means of symbolic notation had as a further consequence the replacement of an irreversible time-axis by a symbolic space, the two-dimensional space of a music manuscript. Without this step from an art of time into a symbolically encoded art of space, not only would 'composition' be impossible (at least as we have understood it for the last millennium), but also the highly acrobatic arts of counterpoint, manifested fully since about the time of Perotinus, would be unthinkable. These techniques forced the composers of ars antiqua not only in the direction of further rationalisation of their notational symbols, but also increasingly —

---

1. Denis Stevens, "Ars Antiqua" in: *The Pelican History of Music*, vol. 1, London 1960, p. 211.
2. Georg Knepler, *Geschichte als Weg zum Musikverständnis*, Leipzig 1977, pp. 205–250.

think of Petrus de Cruce—in the direction of 'top-to-bottom' constructions, which led both to a divisive segmentation of time and, finally, to imposing periodicity on the flow of time, leading in turn to the modern bar system towards the end of the Renaissance.

Monteverdi retrospectively characterised the period of late mediaeval polyphony as prima prattica, seeing his own work as witness of an emerging seconda prattica, which in fact announced the era of an instrumental 'music of representation', and tonality as an adequate syntax for this music. In the course of this second phase, the 'vertical' dimension of musical-symbolic space becomes consolidated, resulting in a new sound-world whose material foundation is the 'purification' of instrumental sound (especially that of wind instruments), with its overtone-structure much more to the fore than is the case with vocal sound. Zarlino had already rationalised a system of chordal connections in the 16th century, and this system was subsequently inserted step by step into the 'new sound'. This process began with the brief cadential formulae of Giovanni Gabrieli, and only generations later arrived at a state we would call 'tonality'. In its clearest manifestation, tonality first came into its own in the generation of Mozart, although already in the music of the French Revolution the first degenerative symptoms of this harmonic idyll announce themselves. The proportion of noise within the sound rises, and finally the harmonic structure takes on hypertrophic tendencies to the point where, at the beginning of the twentieth century, the entire system implodes. Whereas tonality had previously fulfilled an all-encompassing syntactic function, instrumental composition in the 20th century has been able merely to produce private systems. Even Schoenberg's dodecaphony is such a system, despite its wide dissemination during a certain period, not least because it was unable to achieve a mediation between the 'sonic' and syntactic levels. Busoni in his Aesthetic[3] pointed already in 1907 to the increasing contradiction between instrumental sound and complex harmonies, as well as to the increasing redundancy of musical structure: "Our tonal domain has become so narrow, and its expressive forms so stereo-

---

3. Ferruccio Busoni, *Entwurf einer neuen Ästhetik der Tonkunst, Zweite erweiterte Ausgabe*, Leipzig (undated), p. 34f.

typed, that these days no motif exists which would not fit with another known motif so that they could be performed simultaneously."[4] Instrumental music will labour under this redundancy for as long as it remains an independent genre, for every so-called compositional system of the 20th century is no more than a private distribution system. Until now, musicology has not even noticed the problem, since it stops short at notes and graphics...

At the time when Busoni was targeting the historical constipation of the music of the seconda prattica, the initial theoretical and practical steps towards a terza prattica had already been taken. Not only had Richard Pohl pointed to the perspectives of an 'electric music' in his Acoustical Letters of 1853 (!)[5], but at the beginning of the 20th century Thaddeus Cahill had already caused a stir with his 'Dynamophone', a gigantic electric sound-generator whose construction was based upon the theories of Helmholtz. Thus, 150 years ago the desire already existed to realise frequency-combinations able to function, on the level of sound, as 'chords' no longer based in tonality. At the outset it appeared that a new musical paradigm, not yet quite conscious of itself, was attempting to help the old one out of its impasse: new, synthetic sound material as the basis of limitless new harmonies. Historical tendencies often set themselves against the insights of their originators, and although the ideas of a 'pitch-based' electric music have haunted the entire 20th century, it rapidly became evident that they are no more than the prolongation of the historical impasse. The desired new sound would have totally different foundations and aim at totally different morphologies. When Varèse formulated this problem for the first time, a step had been taken in a new direction, that of a definitive break from the ways of thinking which characterise the representational music of the bourgeois era. Referring to the natural philosopher J.M.Hoëne-Wronski and his formulation of an 'intelligence inherent to the sounds', Varèse developed the concept of a kinetic sound, in diametrical opposition to the 'objective' sound of the tradition.

---

4. Busoni, *loc. cit.*, p. 33.
5. Richard Pohl, Seventh Letter: "Physical and Chemical Music", in: *Akustische Briefe*, Leipzig 1853, pp. 95–117.

This 'objective' sound has had a long history, developing along parallel pathways, in terms of its symbolic (and thus reductionist) representation and of the 'purification' of the sound-objects themselves. A point was reached where such a state of 'objectivity' was achieved that these objects could be deployed by composers as the letters of the alphabet might be used when writing a text. Varèse's concept, on the other hand, began from the singular sound as a dynamically-evolving 'process', which implied that the attention of the composer must become completely directed towards the articulation of this process.[6] What Varèse characterised as 'liberation of sound', 'spatial music' and above all as 'organised sound',[7] required, already in the first decades of the previous century, such a radical revolution in musical thought that the seismic shocks have not calmed down to this day. Composition of sound might in itself not be so insurmountably difficult, although if one goes no further than this, what is produced is at most an effect and nowhere near a composition. Varèse formulated his prognosis at a time of all-embracing musical conservatism, the twenties and thirties of the previous century, when neo-classicism was such a dominant doctrine that even Schoenberg leaned towards it in his 12-tone works. The power of this doctrine was such that it drew the new productive force of electricity almost completely into its orbit. Witnesses to this tendency include the numerous electric instruments, from Trautonium to Ondes Martenot, which composers, guided by outdated paradigms, attempted to integrate into the orchestra as enrichments of its sound, and ended up using for soloistic functions when this strategy failed. There is nothing unique about such a volte-face. It was certainly not the first attempt to employ highly-developed technology for conservative purposes. More recently, the new electric productive force would itself generate such conservatism: much electric dance music has achieved nothing more than bringing the spirit of Nazi march music or Carmina Burana up to speed: it is so to speak the internalisation of a Taylorist rhythm of labour within the long-indus-

---

6. See: Fernand Ouellette, *Edgard Varèse*, Paris 1966, p. 27ff, and: Odile Vivier, *Varèse*, Paris 1973, p. 58ff.
7. See: Louise Varèse, *Varèse—A Looking Glass Diary*, New York 1972, p. 42.

trialised domain of 'leisure time'. By the way, it is piquant to observe that interest in electric instruments came only from composers in the (post)impressionist and neoclassical camps (Ravel, Stravinsky, Messiaen, Hindemith) while the 'Vienna School' gave not even a nod in this direction.

Towards the end of the 1940s, a new phase in the development of an authentic electric music could begin upon a totally new basis. This step involved an uncoupling from the idea of an 'instrument', just as modern public transport once dissociated itself from the horse-drawn carriage. The unity of sound-production and sound-diffusion which is so typical of instruments was disrupted in favour of another scheme, namely that of sound recording and sound fixation. Here the diffusion became a separate act, in which the composition was no longer realised in sound but was already realised when made to sound. This is a crucial difference, because it radically alters the position which the composer had occupied in the production process for around a thousand years. The symbolic notation was no longer a mediator: it became instead a technical realisation guide for the composer himself, or an a posteriori embodiment for interested listeners, in other words a by-product. The elimination of the symbolic level forces the composer into a radical reassessment of himself. This process is as yet far from completion.

For, at least during the first years of 'musique concrète' or 'electronic music', it seemed as if their composers intended to incorporate this new music without further ado into the norms of bourgeois representational music. The consequences were not only those gruesomely ascetic loudspeaker concerts of the 1950s, but also the newly-awoken desire of the young composers of the time to design new compositional systems analogous to those of contemporaneous instrumental music. They pinned their hopes on a serialisation of 'electronic music' which would be able to raise the new compositional techniques to a level they had been unable to develop within the confines of instrumental music. The historic quarrel between musique concrète and 'electronic music' had its origins in this (serial) doctrine. Since musically irrelevant mathematical of other scientific disciplines began increasingly to intrude upon this form of serialisation, Pierre Schaeffer began to develop his critique of 'a priori music', which eventually became the starting point for his *Treatise on Musical Objects*.[8] The representatives of 'electronic'-serial music in their turn accused the protagonists of musique concrète of a lack of compositorial conviction.

Such guerrilla warfare is part of the arts business. It can be refreshing, but for the most part fails to address the crux of the problem. In our case, the crux lies not in 'pro' or 'contra' serial techniques, but in the failure of these techniques to adapt to specific new material. The serial method suffers from an antinomy which it is in no position to solve. On the one hand, one can use serial techniques to generate an almost infinite series of values, but this series is in any case too large to even approach being shown off to meaningful advantage within a single composition. For this reason, all composers have derived their own personal rules of implementation from the serial method, which one could at best regard as Modi and which are to a great extent voluntarist. Since serial techniques have historically arisen from a pseudo-spatialisation of symbolic notation, they can only function on the basis of a strict reductionism. This other side of the coin leads to all parametric values having to be standardised, in order to bring mutually discernible values into the field of perception, which one could compare to the 'oppositions' of phonetics. The original pretension of the 'integral' serial method in instrumental music fails in this respect: to integrate instrumental 'timbre' into an even halfway evident series is a senseless and impossible undertaking. The application of serial principles to the new forms of electric sound-production could thus only succeed at the cost of a radical reductionism. The desire to penetrate to the 'atoms' of sound, and to conduct serial forms of sound synthesis upon them, could only be realised with naked sine-tones, if one were to synchronise them, so to speak, into sound-mixtures within the narrow framework of Helmholtz's theories. That those theories themselves represented a (culturally determined) reductionism, in which complex noises played no role, did not disturb composers until they noticed that while absolutely any (serial) intervallic relations could be involved

---

8. Pierre Schaeffer, *Traité des objets musicaux*, Paris 1966.

in sine-tone mixtures, the resulting sounds always had the same stereotyped character. Stockhausen's two early electronic studies bear witness to this. Aesthetically speaking they are more advertisements for the new genre than works of musical art.

As long as horizontal sound synthesis — that is to say, the composition of sound out of successive particles — was serially organised, it led to end-results whose aesthetic quality the composer was unable to predict (and which might quite often have surprised him). Here too, synthesis could not proceed from a sonic idea, but merely from the proportions between these particles, from which the eventual sound-gestalt, that is to say the object of perception, could scarcely or not at all be predetermined. Where, on the other hand, composers transposed or distributed 'concrete' sounds according to serial methods, the contradictions became glaringly obvious: the pounding of a steam-locomotive, captured within a scale from which a serial melody might possibly be extracted, is no more than a blatant subjection of the terza prattica under the norms of the seconda prattica. And furthermore, a transposition on music paper is fundamentally different from a transposition on tape. On the paper, symbols are displaced in abstract space and the instrumentalist plays another note. Transposing with tape (or computer) causes a concrete alteration in the sonic material: such transposition is therefore a deformation, which is often accompanied by the risk of Mickey Mouse effects. None of this has anything in common with Schoenberg's ideal of a *Klangfarbenmelodie* (timbral melody).

It took centuries before the vertical sound-formations inherent to European pitch-scales — the chords — could be disposed syntactically in such a way that their concatenation seemed evident or even as 'second nature' to the perception. With timbres everything looks totally different: they know of no ordering by scales, and accordingly cannot be integrated into any conventionally syntactical 'system'. Their mutual 'sympathy or antipathy' — to use Descartes' term — can at most be suggested in vague psychological terms; measuring them remains entirely a matter for the subjective discretion of the composer. Only where sounds are from the outset highly standardised into a small number of categories is it possible to integrate them with conventional formal strategies.

But are those strategies actually what we have in mind? Whereas historically 'electronic music' trusted in a serial mediation between its ingredients, musique concrète has concentrated to a great extent on the development of narrative formal structures. In the current situation, such structures seem to be the most fertile basis for the development of new spaces for the imagination. However, it is still not possible to formalise them.

Where the most diverse forms of electric music have incorporated realistic sounds borrowed from the outside world, a new contradiction arrives on the scene. It is that between the semantic meaning of such sounds and their musical disposition. Wherever composers of former centuries have included 'naturalistic' elements in their compositions (think of the *battaglia* pieces of the 16th century, or Liszt's *Mazeppa* or Saint-Saëns's *Danse macabre*), these were depicted within the confines of the available musical means. Only Wellington's Victory, Beethoven's one-man battle of nations against Napoleon, is a serious exception to this, on account of the real cannons, regarding which Gottfried Weber stated already in 1825 that here was a case of "stepping outside the proper domain of the art of music"[9]. Where such 'stepping outside' became fundamental to the musical structure of musique concrète and its successors, two diachronic levels of perception were addressed. The musical level is activated along the flow of discourse of the music itself; the other, semantic level however leads the consciousness constantly to other (extramusical) areas, upon which it dwells for durations independent of those of the musical textures. This is so to speak the inversion of cinema, where the sound-effects merely support or intensify the completely concrete visual images. Such a comparison already begs the question of whether electric music as a whole is as out of place in a concert hall as Monteverdi's *Orfeo* would have been in a church 400 years ago.

The development of independent narrative structures seems like child's play when it leans upon visual or literary models. However, it becomes damnably complicated when it must integrate an

---

9. Gottfried Weber, "Über Tonmalerei", in: Stefan Kunze (ed.), *Ludwig van Beethoven — die Werke im Spiegel seiner Zeit*, Laaber 1987, p. 285.

already semantically-weighted material into completely new musical structures: this is a matter of mediating between multiple levels simultaneously. Much electric music which has operated with 'concrete' samples has totally failed in the face of this multiplicity. This failure displays itself with especial clarity in that type of work where sequences of (often oh so 'profound') text are imposed upon the sounds, while the relationship between the composer's philosophical insights and the sounds remains completely intangible. This takes us not one step further than the 18th century melodramas of Benda or Rousseau. In view of this type of hybrid result, the question of to what extent electric music is not just a new musical genre but simply a new art form remains as relevant as ever. In this respect electric music might be compared with the art of film — some French colleagues speak indeed of *cinéma pour l'oreille* — which from technical, dramaturgical and aethetic points of view is something completely different from theatre. Both new art forms have in common that their terrain is wider than that of their historical predecessors. As for electric music, we can conclude that its relations with the outside world requires changes which are just as radical as those needed in the construction of its inner structure. I hardly need to emphasise that both of these exist in a dialectical relationship in every art. But the quality of that relationship changes radically in so far as electric music — on the basis of its specific material — can no longer appeal to the autonomous status of historical art music. Possibly this loss of autonomy, which also stands all traditional answers to the question of 'meaning' on their heads, can be considered as the heaviest pressure lying on the shoulders of the terza prattica, which thus forces it to consider playing a completely new aesthetic and social role.

This returns us once more to the principle of narrative. But what in fact is a (musical or dramatic) narrative structure? It is a concentration of reality, rather than a reduction. Concentration aims at the emergence of substance, while reduction would achieve merely a formalisation of the mode of appearance of reality. Take for example the royal dramas of Shakespeare: their battle scenes embody a concentration of all actions, gestures, thoughts and motives to their essence, rather than a formalistic reduction.

Take Beethoven's techniques of translation, in the etymological sense of 'carrying over': his Fifth Symphony does not present a 'tone-painting' of the historical aspirations of the bourgeois class of its time, neither does it present a formal reduction, which indeed would have been impossible. Its task of concentration begins with the invention of specific intonations, which subsequently fulfill the function of indices within a purely musical context. We cannot take over models from such dramaturgies, but we can even today learn a great deal from their strategies of translation.

However the new art of sound might be constituted, it cannot avoid — simultaneously with a reconsideration of its dramaturgical foundations — coming to terms with the specific problems of its material. Neither scientific-acoustical criteria nor advances in computer technology offer the slightest assistance here. Acoustics and perceptual psychology have long offered such contradictory results that nothing of compositional relevance may be expected of them, above all because (experimental) acoustics is itself a reductionist science. On the other hand, even the most advanced computer technology is in no position to offer a contribution to the inner structural coherence of the new art of sound. Computer programs model sounds according to the insights of their programmers. They contribute to the standardisation of often very brilliant sounds, but give not the slightest answer to any aesthetic problems. This could be the reason why musical computer technology searches desperately for pseudo-solutions, and settles for example upon nonsensical notions such as 'live-music' or even 'interactive real-time composition', by means of which it does nothing more in fact than elevate musical performance modalities onto the altar of composition techniques: works are in this way degraded to 'events' and the concert to a 'performance', which does no more than demonstrate the efficiency of hard- and software, exactly as traders are accustomed to do in the centres of the commodity economy — with much hollow rhetoric.

Pierre Schaeffer came to the point of this problem in his *Traité*. The culturally domesticated sounds of the vocal/instrumental epoch functioned so to speak as faits accomplis, which would be woven into musical textures by composers. However, as soon as we immerse ourselves in the micro-world of a single sound, we are confronted by two problems. Firstly, no (natural) sound obeys the abstract formulae or laws of the acousticians. If the composer wishes somehow to achieve anything with the structure of a particular sound, he must — each time anew — analyse the components of this sound with the greatest precision. This kind of work differs in every respect from that of traditional composers. Many a classical composer could rejoice over a good clarinettist or be annoyed by a bad one; nevertheless he composed for 'the' clarinet. This generalisation exists no longer for the composer of electric music: to him, each sound is a special case, and perhaps the following rule could be formulated: the stricter the (cultural) selection of sounds, the better the chance of an evident syntax; the weaker the selection (and therefore the larger the abundance of sounds at our disposal), the smaller the chance of such a syntax. Only specific narrative structures can provide here for a preselection of sound-materials. The second problem deals directly with composition itself. In cases where sounds have become kinetic, having been elevated from the micro- to the macro-level, listening should, indeed must, obviously concentrate on what happens within the sound. In so far as a composition consists of more than one sound, the problem also arises of the meaningful interweaving of those multidimensional sounds, whose complex course has, one hopes, been carefully articulated. This problem of new time-levels becomes increasingly acute where — as I have already suggested — there are actually no adequate structures within which those new sounds could be embedded. Almost all contemporary electric compositions beat around the bush regarding these fundamental problems. The more brilliant the sound-synthesis programs of the computer world become, the greater becomes the danger that composers allow themselves to be seduced by the glamour of the resulting sounds, so that they are hardly interested any longer in a compositional or narrative mediation between them. This situation has delivered those myriads of electric compositions in which the sounds float around in a noncommittal way like fat globules in soup.

I have tried to outline some of the fundamental problems which accompany the birth-pangs of the terza prattica. These are all problems which are not to be solved by mere technological means. They rather need a radical new aesthetic orientation, of which the entire contemporary music world is apparently no longer capable. Such a reorientation, which must seize, so to speak, both the inner and outer worlds of electric music, is not something that happens from one day to the next. Nevertheless it is a necessary historical process, without which what was still avant-garde yesterday will already be arts and crafts by tomorrow. We become accustomed to nothing so quickly as a new sound, especially when it continues to float around in an aesthetic nirvana. What was previously characteristic of the breakthoughs of the prima prattica and the seconda prattica is no less valid for the historical perspectives of a terza prattica: there can be no new artforms without a new understanding of the world, without an understanding of a new world.

PERSONALIA

JONATHAN DUNSBY

Jonathan Dunsby is Professor at the University of Reading, department of Music. He formerly taught at Kings College London and the University of Southern California. He studied piano with Fanny Waterman and won prizes in various international competitions. He then concentrated on work as an accompanist, including recitals and broadcasts with violinist Vanya Milanova. He is the author of *Structural Ambiguity in Brahms*, and the Cambridge Music Handbook *Schoenberg: Pierrot lunaire*, and co-author with Arnold Whittall of *Music Analysis in Theory and Practice*. In 1981–86 he was Founding Editor of the journal "Music Analysis", and he has contributed musicological and theoretical articles to many books and leading journals. He edited and contributed to the volume *Early Twentieth-Century Music*. Since 2001 he has been an international advisory member of the Andante Academy.

Professor Dunsby has given lectures and lecture-recitals throughout the USA, in Brazil, and in various European countries. His book *Performing Music: Shared Concerns* has been widely influential. Recent research includes chapters for Cambridge University Press books on music theory, on the history of 19th-century music, and on performance studies, as well as chapters for the Einaudi Encyclopaedia on Texture and on Analysis and Performance. His latest book *Making Words Sing*, a study of aspects of text-setting in 19th- and 20th-century music, has appeared in 2003.

JOSEPH N. STRAUS

Joseph N. Straus, Professor at Queens College and the Graduate Center (PhD, Yale), is a music theorist specializing in music of the twentieth century, with research interests that include set theory, voice-leading in post-tonal music, the music of Stravinsky, and the music of Ruth Crawford Seeger. His book *Introduction to Post-Tonal Theory* is a standard college textbook on this topic. His book *Remaking the Past* received the Wallace Berry award from the Society for Music Theory (SMT). Prof. Straus was the President of the SMT from 1997–99.

Representative publications are: *Stravinsky's Late Music*; *Introduction to Post-Tonal Theory*; *The Music of Ruth Crawford Seeger*; *Anthology of Music by Women for Study and Analysis*; *Remaking the Past: Musical Modernism and the Influence of the Tonal Tradition*; and *Milton Babbitt: Words About Music* (co-editor).

Personalia

YVES KNOCKAERT

Yves Knockaert is Professor of music history, philosophy of music and contemporary music at the Lemmens Institute in Leuven, and at the Queen Elisabeth College of Music. He is also guest professor at the Department of Audiovisual and Plastic Art of the Karel de Grote-Hogeschool in Antwerp. Since 1997 he is a member of the pedagogic and artistic committee of the Orpheus Institute.

He is the author of many programs on 20th-century music for Belgian Radio, and is a member of the board of editors of the music journal "Contra.". He has contributed to several specialized journals, wrote the book *Wendingen* (Turns), about drastic changes in 20th-century music, and several "Muziekcahiers" on historical and sociological topics. *Muziek uit de voorbije eeuw* (Music from the past century), a collection of essays by Yves Knockaert and the Belgian composer Boudewijn Buckinx, was published in 1999.

MAX PADDISON

Max Paddison is Professor of Music at the University of Durham. He studied composition and piano at the Royal Manchester College of Music, musicology at the University of Exeter, and, on a DAAD scholarship, did research on the philosophy and sociology of music of Theodor Adorno at the Johann Wolfgang Goethe University, Frankfurt/Main. His publications include *Adorno's Aesthetics of Music*; *Adorno, Modernism and Mass Culture*; *Musique contemporaine: Perspectives théoriques et philosophiques*, jointly edited with Irène Deliège; and articles in "Journal of the Royal Musical Association", "Music Analysis", "Popular Music", "Tempo", "The British Journal of Aesthetics", "Musik & Ästhetik", and the *New Grove Dictionary of Music and Musicians*. Recent publications include essays in *Adorno: A Critical Reader*; *The Cambridge Companion to Adorno*; *The Cambridge Companion to Stravinsky*; and *The Cambridge History of Nineteenth-Century Music*. A composer in a previous incarnation, he won the Royal Philharmonic Prize for Composition in 1967. He still occasionally composes, but sees himself now as a scholar working in the field of critical theory, aesthetics, philosophy and sociology of music.

KONRAD BOEHMER

Konrad Boehmer was born in 1941 in Berlin. He studied composition with Gottfried Michael Koenig (1959–61) and philosophy, sociology and musicology at the University of Cologne, writing his doctoral thesis on the theory of open form in new music (*Zur Theorie der offenen Form in der neuen Musik*). From 1961–1963 he was active at the electronic music studios of the WDR (West German Broadcasting Company) in Cologne. In 1966 he moved to the Netherlands and worked until 1968 at the Institute of Sonology at Utrecht University. He then became music editor of the Dutch weekly newspaper *Vrij Nederland* and in 1972 professor of music history and new music theory at the Royal Conservatory in The Hague, where since 1994 he has been director of the Institute of Sonology.

In the 1970's and '80's he was repeatedly guest professor at the Latin-American Courses for Contemporary Music, as well as extensively in the USA and Europe. — His composition *Information* was presented with the Dutch AVRO-award (1966) and the electronic work *Aspekt* was awarded the first price of the Vth Paris Biennale in 1968. His music drama *Doktor Faustus* was awarded the Rolf-Liebermann prize in 1983. In 1985 the City of Rotterdam awarded him the Pierre-Bayle prize for his writings on music and musical life.

His works include concert music (chamber and symphonic), music theatre and electroacoustic music, and have been featured at major international events.

EDITORS
Frank Agsteribbe, Sylvester Beelaert, Peter Dejans

AUTHORS
Jonathan Dunsby
Joseph N. Straus
Yves Knockaert
Max Paddison
Konrad Boehmer

TRANSLATION
XLNt Communication (Knockaert and Preface)
Richard Barrett (Boehmer)

MUSICAL EXAMPLES
Peter Knockaert

LAY-OUT
Filiep Tacq, Ghent

PRESS
Grafikon, Oostkamp
Bioset, 100gr

ISBN 90 5867 369 3
D/2004/1869/21
NUR 663

© 2004 by Leuven University Press / Universitaire Pers Leuven / Presses Universitaires de Louvain
Blijde-Inkomststraat 5, B-3000 Leuven (Belgium)

All rights reserved.
Except in those cases expressly determined by law,
no part of this publication may be multiplied,
saved in an automated data file or made public in any way whatsoever
without the express prior written consent of the publishers.

www.ingramcontent.com/pod-product-compliance
Lightning Source LLC
Chambersburg PA
CBHW070947180426
43194CB00041B/1711